CATCHING THE
RHYTHM *of* LOVE

Other Books by Neil Clark Warren

Finding Contentment

Finding the Love of Your Life

God Said It, Don't Sweat It

*How to Know If Someone Is Worth
Pursuing in Two Dates or Less*

Learning to Live with the Love of Your Life

Make Anger Your Ally

CATCHING THE RHYTHM *of* LOVE

Experience Your Way to a Spectacular Marriage

NEIL CLARK WARREN, PH.D.

THOMAS NELSON PUBLISHERS®
Nashville

This book is gratefully dedicated to
Richard A. Hogan, my first mentor
in psychology, and to Ferne Warren Hogan,
my sister, who cared for me so generously
when I was growing up.

Copyright © 2000 by Neil Clark Warren

Published in Nashville, Tennessee, by Thomas Nelson, Inc.

Scripture quotations noted NLT are from the *Holy Bible,* New Living Translation, copyright © 1996. Used by permission of Tyndale House Publishers, Inc., Wheaton, Illinois 60189. All rights reserved.

Scripture quotations noted TLB are from *The Living Bible,* copyright © 1971. Used by permission of Tyndale House Publishers, Inc., Wheaton, Illinois. All rights reserved.

Library of Congress Cataloging-in-Publication Data
Warren, Neil Clark.
    Catching the rhythm of Love : experience your way to a spectacular marriage / Neil Clark Warren
        p. cm.
    ISBN 0-7852-7344-1 (hc)
    1. Marriage. 2. Love. I. Title.

HQ734.W3174 2000
306.81—dc21   00-030539
                                                                          CIP

Printed in the United States of America.
1 2 3 4 5 6 — 05 04 03 02 01 00

contents

acknowledgments

I have a reputation for bouncing psychological ideas and theories off my friends, clients, and colleagues, and they always respond with ideas and theories of their own. So in a way, this book is a joint effort. I owe countless persons a debt of gratitude for all the ways they have contributed to my thinking and motivated my best effort.

My closest friends have been involved with me in this blending of ideas for more than thirty years. Three mornings a week, I go to a gym to work out with Howard J. Privett. Sometimes, we talk as much as we lift. His influence on me through the years has been incalculable. Rick Thyne, a psychotherapist himself, and I, on the other hand, have eaten lunch together every other Thursday through all these years. We never hesitate discussing our most recent discoveries in the areas of psychotherapy and life. Clifford Penner and I have been partners for thirty years, and we stop and chat throughout virtually every working day as we move from our mutual waiting room to our individual offices. These three persons have made an enormous difference in my life.

My clients have, I suppose, taught me the most about

how to make a marriage better. In a way, I have been their pupil for several hours each week. They have shared their frustrations and their victories, and together we have usually ended up celebrating the latter together.

I talk about these clients throughout this book, but I want to make it clear that I have disguised their stories so that they are not identifiable. However, these are the stories I have heard from week to week in the privacy of my office.

I want to mention briefly three other people who have contributed to this effort. Sue Braden, my administrative assistant, knows how to make decisions for me as well as I do, and she has made thousands of them. Greg Forgatch, the president of eharmony, our marital matching organization, has constantly motivated me to think harder and more carefully.

And special appreciation is reserved for Keith Wall, my editor and friend. This is our sixth effort together, and I am the delighted recipient of his highly professional assistance. I am grateful for his careful attention to this manuscript.

I should tell you, though, that no list of acknowledgments would ever be complete for me without mentioning my wife, Marylyn. As this manuscript regularly attests, she has had more to do with this volume than any other I have written. Literally no one could have gotten inside my heart the way she has, and the newness and creativity represented by this book have more to do with my relationship with Marylyn than with anyone else.

introduction

Move Your Marriage from Mediocrity to Magnificence

I assume it's time for your marriage to become significantly more satisfying and fulfilling, and reading this book may be the impetus you need to upgrade your relationship from mediocre to magnificent. Perhaps you've been yearning for, maybe even praying for, something dramatic to happen between you and your partner that will create momentum—something that will propel your marriage into a new orbit. This book is designed to give you a marital growth spurt that will move you forward and fill you with more hope than you've had for years.

Making marriage enjoyable and meaningful for *both* spouses is not easy, and I'm painfully aware of the overwhelming marital failure rate in our society. But what I fear most for you is a loss of hope. When so many of your friends and acquaintances have given up on their marriages, you might be tempted to follow their example. And even if you don't give up, you might opt to settle for whatever state your marriage is in right now. I don't recommend either one of these options. If you read this book, you and your spouse will be the proud owners of new marital assets: a lot more hope and enthusiasm for your marriage, and an abundance of practical, proven ideas for making your relationship better and better. If you and your partner apply the principles outlined in this book, you will be on your way to catching the rhythm of love.

Fortunately, marriage doesn't have to be perfect to be pleasing and delightful. You don't have to build the ideal relationship to experience deep-down satisfaction. *All you need is a clear sense that you're moving relentlessly toward your goal.* Hope flourishes when both desire and expectancy are strong. I'm assuming that you already have the desire for a great marriage, and this book supplies the tools for turning expectations into reality.

Don't Put This Book Down Until You're Finished!

Follow my logic: *you* want a better marriage. You may even be desperate for a better marriage. But you aren't sure how to achieve it. So you pick up this book.

I claim to have a plan that will make your marriage better. I promise that when you finish this book, your marriage will be poised to move from so-so to spectacular, from ordinary to extraordinary. So don't dawdle! Get reading!

"Aha," you say, "but how do *I* know if *you* know what you're talking about? Why should I believe you have the insights to make *our* marriage better?"

Fair enough. Without tooting my horn too much, let me list my qualifications in one paragraph. I've been a clinical psychologist for more than three decades, and I've worked with every imaginable marital challenge—no doubt many of them a lot like yours. I've researched marriage and marital counseling from dozens of perspectives. I've written several relationship books and countless journal articles about marriage. I've spoken about marriage throughout the world, and I've been interviewed about marriage on more than two thousand radio and television programs. Finally, and maybe most important, I've been happily married for forty years, and my wife and I have three daughters who are happily married.

If you bring a burning need for a better marriage, and if I bring years of professional experience, our connection with each other may be exactly what you need. Perhaps your marriage has become progressively worse in the last few months or even years. And maybe you're on the verge of tossing in the towel. I'm not terribly concerned with what *hasn't* worked before. I'm just glad that you have this book in your hands right now, that you and I have these moments together. I know that between us we can get your marriage growing.

How Much Growth Can Your Marriage Achieve in the Next Twelve Months?

Obviously, I don't know the details of your particular situation. But regardless of your circumstances, I'm confident you can improve the quality of your marriage by at least 10 percent within the next year. If you do, your relationship will be infused with hope and optimism. When your marriage gets 10 percent better in any twelve-month period, the chance of its improving another 10 percent in the following twelve months becomes very high. Growth produces positive momentum; the more you grow, the more likely it is that you will grow even more.

I encourage married people to keep their expectations reasonable. You might long for a marital miracle that would change everything about your relationship, but this doesn't happen often. If you expect your marriage to be storybook perfect immediately, you're likely to be discouraged with much more modest gains.

Focus on this: if your marriage improves by 10 percent each year, imagine how enchanting and enjoyable your relationship will be five years from now. Don't stop there. Look ahead ten or fifteen years. Talk about a magnificent marriage!

Four Principles for Making Your Marriage Better

If you want your marriage to become progressively stronger, four psychological principles will give you an immediate head start.

First, you need to become crystal clear about your goals. What *exactly* do you want your marriage to become? I frequently ask couples what they want their relationship to look like after we've finished marriage counseling, and they often talk in vague generalities. One spouse might say, "Well, I guess I'd like us to be much more romantic and affectionate," or "Our goal is to fight less and enjoy each other more." This is like going to the car dealership and telling the salesman you want a vehicle with an engine and four wheels. When it comes to marriage, you must dream a precise dream, and you must spell out all your hoped-for changes in detail. Unless you know your exact destination, you're going to expend a lot of time and energy figuring out where you want to go.

Second, change is almost always gradual. Let's face it. People in our society want instantaneous results. We love stories of overnight success. We have become conditioned by television shows that resolve complex problems in a half hour. But in real life, many of the dreams for your marriage will take time. If you expect them to suddenly appear in perfect form, you may wait forever. However, if you begin to recognize pieces of the changes, even in incomplete form, your hope will soar, and your appreciation for progress will make even greater progress more likely.

Third, encouragement is a powerful force for marital progress. When you and your partner begin to see gains in your relationship—even little ones—you must cheer each other on. This positive reinforcement will greatly determine the likelihood of these changes becoming permanent and of more changes adding to them. What's more, how you encourage your mate is vitally important. Some people love to be complimented verbally. Others are elated when you spend more time attending to them. Maybe for others, encouragement comes in the form of tangible rewards—a small gift or a night on the town.

Fourth, everyone responds better to rewards than to punishment. When your marriage doesn't go the way you want it to, punishing your partner never helps. You're not going to get positive results by yelling at your spouse, issuing threats, giving the silent treatment, criticizing, or badgering. Needless to say, hitting, pushing, dominating, or demeaning is a sure way to drown—not rescue—your marriage.

Why I Believe My Approach Is Innovative

Over the past several decades, psychology, psychiatry, and other mental health disciplines have focused on a problem-centered approach. Practitioners in these fields usually try to identify what's wrong and then set about fixing it. If you were to consult a counselor, one of the first things you would likely hear is: "Now, tell me what's wrong with your marriage."

This is what I call the *mechanic's method*. What happens when you hear a strange noise under the hood of your car? You take your sputtering vehicle to the mechanic, who runs diagnostic tests, determines the problem, and replaces the faulty part. But people are not automobiles, and relationships cannot be fixed by replacing parts! That's why the problem-centered approach to marriage counseling frequently fails.

Recently, a friend of mine named Andrew tried to explain why he and his wife got divorced. "When our marriage became seriously troubled," he said, "my wife and I started therapy. We went for twenty sessions or so, and every session made our relationship worse."

I was tempted to defend my profession, but I've heard similar stories enough to know they're too common. "Why was it so unhelpful?" I asked.

"Our therapy consisted of cataloging our problems and zeroing in on them one by one," Andrew said.

"So, what happened?" I said.

"It was a bloodbath!" he nearly shouted. "We dissected each problem in excruciating detail. We talked endlessly about our flaws and failings. By the end of the sessions, my wife and I felt like heavyweight boxers who had just gone twelve rounds. But here's the worst part: during the week, our wounds would heal a little bit, and then we'd go back the next week and tear each other's scabs off. The bloodletting would begin all over again. We seldom spoke to each other on the way home, and we fumed and stewed for days."

Andrew concluded by saying, "Our therapy didn't make us feel hopeful. It made us feel hopeless."

This is no way to strengthen marriages! And it has to stop! I'm convinced that we're losing thousands of marriages in America every year because of some well-intentioned but misguided professional efforts to expose and air all the marital problems and deficits. Doing this usually results in pain crashing over a couple like a tsunami while their love sinks to the depths of the sea.

Of course, problems must be dealt with eventually, but not when the marriage is withered and emaciated, and not until the marriage has received some badly needed nutrients. Once this happens, the marriage won't have so many problems.

The first innovative principle in this book is this: you give your marriage maximum opportunity to grow if you feed it, nurture it, and strengthen it before you start delving into your problems. If your marriage is hurting, be very careful about pursuing any therapeutic approach that forces you to obsess over each other's weaknesses, deficiencies, and shortcomings. You're liable to end up with a marriage that is more wounded after treatment than before.

Second, more than any other reason, marriages improve because two people regularly share positive, bonding experiences. There are thousands of experiences that can weld the two of you together. Some people read books together, others travel to faraway places, and still others play tennis. The crucial ingredient is that both partners share these experiences at a deep level.

Third, this book introduces what I consider to be a critical technique for fortifying a marriage—what I refer to as *focus of consciousness*. I will discuss this in great detail, but here is what it amounts to: when two people learn to focus their thinking and feeling so that they center on the same thing, they become bonded together in that moment. If consciousness includes at its center a place for the mate—thoughts, wishes, needs—the bonding will be lasting. If you and your partner have ever wept together during a movie, held each other tightly as you watched a sunset, or squeezed each other's hand during a concert, you know about this concept.

Fourth, this book puts a whole new spin on several traditional topics. For instance, every marriage expert in America talks about conflict resolution. I am all for resolving conflicts, but I have become progressively concerned about the timing of the resolution. Frankly, when conflict is allowed to go beyond an hour or two, it becomes like Parmesan cheese stuck on the dirty dishes in your sink. Let it harden, and you can hardly wash it off. But if you catch it early, it's easy to remove. And that's why I will tell you about *rapid-fire conflict resolution,* which prevents conflicts from solidifying.

Finally, this book is new and different because it is positive. The time has come for us to adopt an upbeat attitude about marital change. The time has come for us to recognize that treating each other with dignity, warmth, and kindness will produce a wholly different marital atmosphere. The time has come for us to recognize that making marriage work is the single greatest thing we will ever do on this earth.

One Last Personal Word

Every single word in this book is the result of my reflecting on years of marital-revitalization efforts. I have tried to take the best of what I've learned from thousands of clinical hours and make it easily accessible to you. I have an intense desire for your marriage to become more satisfying, rewarding, and gratifying. If it does, everything about your place in the world will be better. And your family will benefit from the effort as well.

Right now, the single most important thing for you to focus on is the strengthening of your love relationship. I've watched it happen thousands of times for couples. It's critical that it happen one more time for you and the love of your life.

1

A Lighter
Touch Can Transform
Your Marriage

As a clinical psychologist for the past thirty-five years, I have consulted with literally thousands of married people. My aim has always been to strengthen their marriages, and I have worked my hardest to reach this goal. Recently, I discovered that in many cases, I might have worked *too* hard. I have been astounded by a new approach to marital growth that clearly reduces the role of work and emphasizes a lighter touch.

As crazy as it may sound, marriages have often become less fulfilling precisely because they have been worked at so hard. That is, some marriages have been poked and prodded, studied and scrutinized, examined and explored to a degree that may be counterproductive. My colleagues and I have conducted clinical research on marital health for decades, and we recently completed a major national study of eight hundred marriages—both strong ones and troubled ones. I have become convinced that the secret to making your marriage progressively better involves taking some of the load off it.

This book spells out a set of principles for lightening up on your marriage—letting it grow by feeding it well and treating it with enormous dignity.

Marital health is fundamentally determined by the robustness of the love that two people have for each other. Love soars on the wings of shared experiences that are inspirational, humorous, exciting, or hopeful. Married people who share experiences like these are more likely to feel romantically attracted to each other. But psychologists, psychiatrists, and other mental health workers have often clung to misguided notions about how to maximize these romantic experiences. Without knowing it, we have frequently minimized a couple's love life by pinching and squeezing their focus onto "critical issues"—all the weaknesses, shortcomings, and deficits. We have worked them to death on problem solving, and with our "professional" approach, we have frequently left them to die from a lack of joyful and meaningful mutual experiences.

All this is to say that marriages are crying out for a lighter touch. I have become convinced that this lighter approach is crucial to the health, strength, and well-being of any marital relationship. The time has come for a relaxation of our obsessive concentration on problems and pitfalls. Let's celebrate what's wonderful about our relationships, how they can most effectively catch a breeze and sail forward, how spouses can nurture their love and positive feelings.

My experience is that this approach frequently results in a symphonic marital sound. This sound tends to be rich in timbre and vibrancy. Harmony, rhythm, and an upbeat tempo enrich your relationship incredibly.

Let me show you how to catch the rhythm of love. Give me these next pages to convince you that this new approach has revolutionary power for your marriage. If you come to believe that I'm right, I guarantee that your marriage will be on the verge of explosive growth. All the exertion you've thought was necessary to make your marriage healthy will be replaced by shared experiences that entertain, inspire, encourage, and deepen your love for each other.

What's Right with Your Marriage?

I counseled a couple, Jason and Cheryl, who had been married six years when they made an appointment to see me. The first five years of their marriage had been fulfilling and satisfying, but the last one had been dismal. Jason had received a promotion in the software company where he worked, and he put in countless hours of overtime to grasp his new responsibilities and prove himself as a team player. Meanwhile, Cheryl got involved in many activities outside the home. They became more like roommates than lovers, and their communication revolved around all the mundane tasks of life—paying bills, fixing up their house, fulfilling family obligations. Naturally, the emotional closeness they once enjoyed became a memory, and they alternated between fighting fiercely and enduring cold, silent distance.

At our first session, I began by asking, "So, what's *right* with your marriage?"

Both gave me expressions that clearly said, "Huh?" No doubt they had expected me to ask what was *wrong,* and they probably had rehearsed their litany of marital faults and flaws.

I tried again. "I mean, what's going well in your relationship? What do you enjoy about each other? What are the strengths of your marriage?"

Their faces formed question marks, and they sat in silence for a minute. Obviously, they had not thought about their collective attributes for a while.

Finally, Jason said, "Well, we've always enjoyed traveling together. When we go on a trip or weekend getaway, we get back some of the old magic we used to have—at least for a couple of days. And we love to entertain together. We work really well together when we're throwing a party or having guests over."

"Good," I said. "That's the kind of thing I'm looking for. What else?"

As Jason opened his mouth to continue, his wife interrupted. "Dr. Warren, aren't we going to talk about the problems we're struggling with?" Cheryl apparently had her own agenda, and she was incredulous about the direction we were heading. "We've got some significant issues to address, and I don't want to waste our time and yours if we're just going to put sunshine and smiles on everything."

What I explained to Cheryl is what I explain to every couple: "You must absolutely examine and resolve problems in your marriage, especially those that surface repeatedly. But you must approach them with as much optimism and hopefulness as possible. Many couples are so consumed by what's wrong with their relationship that they forget all the things that are right. And when they become so focused on their problems, they stop pursuing the experiences that generate positive feelings and closeness. It becomes a vicious cycle, and soon everything about the relationship looks gloomy and grim."

Almost immediately, we developed a plan for Jason and Cheryl to build on their strengths and share again the experiences that brought out the best in their relationship. Ever so slowly, their emotional distance closed, and some of the warmth returned. This created the kind of optimistic environment in which we could tackle their problems in a spirit of mutual cooperation rather than opposition.

Jason and Cheryl's situation makes my point: I am certainly not suggesting that you avoid problems or sweep contentious issues under the rug. I'm saying not to become so weighed down by your flaws that you can't take steps forward. Lighten up a little, give yourselves a break, refuse to be dominated by your problems—then watch as your relationship gains momentum in a positive direction.

Try Not to Try Too Hard

I've been playing golf for many years now, and I've repeatedly been given two words of advice to improve my game: "Swing easy!" I've heard this admonition often because I'm the kind of golfer who is so intense and uptight that I undermine my success. Every golfer knows that the more relaxed and fluid your swing, the more likely the ball will go straight and far. But when I tee up my ball, I worry about the mechanics of my swing; I tense up and grip the club too tightly; I focus on my deficiencies so much that I overcompensate for them. Therefore, much to my dismay (and my friends' amusement), I slice and hook my ball into the trees, sand traps, and the lake. Swinging easy isn't natural to my thinking. I reason that if swinging easy gets good results, swinging harder should get even better ones. As I repeatedly discover, however, this isn't the case.

Mastering the game of golf is a lot like mastering marriage. What is it, after all, about swinging easy that helps so much? I think it's all about synchrony. And *synchrony* produces *symphony*. For example, when all the parts of your body work together, you experience a combination of intricate physical precision and maximum physical power. We refer to this quality of harmonizing, blending, and flowing as coordination. Let your body find its coordination, and you can hardly believe how powerfully and accurately it can deliver the club head to the ball. The shot will amaze you because it represents the miracle of synchronized effortlessness.

Isn't this exactly what marriages need? We should experience something smooth and refined about our relationships, something akin to silk rubbing against silk rather than metal parts clashing against other metal parts. Our marriages should run with all the sureness and precision of a Swiss watch—with all those intricate gear mechanisms clicking away in perfect rhythm.

As a Husband, I've Been Trying to Swing Easy

My wife, Marylyn, and I worked far too hard on our marriage for decades. My back is nearly broken from trying to shape her into the wife I've always wanted her to be. And I suppose she has developed a double hernia while trying to mold and form me into a decent husband. Like most couples, we had our work cut out for us when we married. We were both greenhorn rookies when we embarked on this challenging endeavor, and we had no training or practice in being good spouses. We labored so hard to improve our deficits, to shore up our shortcomings, that we missed many opportunities to create wonderful experiences together. We toiled so strenuously in ways that seemed unnatural that we actually added a negative tinge to situations where there needn't have been one.

But lately, employing this new, lighter approach, I've watched our marriage grow by leaps and bounds. Let me give you a couple of examples. Marylyn loves to talk, and she likes having me interact with her. She often says that when we talk together, she feels close to me, in love with me, as if she's one with me. Now, I wasn't raised to be a talker. My dad never talked to my mom. Every once in a while he would nod in her direction, grunt a few times, and rustle the newspaper. For him, that was deep conversation. Obviously, I didn't have much training and modeling for marital communication. To make matters worse, I never let on that I was communication impaired. If Marylyn pressed me too hard for meaningful dialogue, I distracted her by focusing the discussion on sex. Sometimes the diversion worked; most often it didn't.

It didn't take a genius to notice that when I failed to communicate deeply, our marriage began to bog down as if we were doing the backstroke in a pool of molasses. She wasn't happy to see me when I got home from work. She never sat close to me. She gave me only stiff, obligatory hugs (the kind with a foot of space between her body and mine). There was no vibrancy in our life together. Now mind you, I don't need all that deep talk to feel in love with her, but boy, without the conversation she wanted with me, her love turned quickly to boredom. I'm embarrassed to admit it took about fifteen or twenty years before I did something about this situation. Obviously, Marylyn needed something from me that I felt unable to provide. And predictably, all the feelings associated with this problem—her constant frustration and unmet needs, my sense of failure and incompetence—threw our already chilly love life into the deep freeze.

I always thought that learning how to talk would require more work than I was capable of. Then came the lighter approach. I decided if she wanted to talk a lot, I'd just let go, be as natural as possible, and get as good at communicating as I could. I stopped worrying about my dialogue deficits. I stopped trying to formulate cogent responses before Marylyn had finished talking. I stopped being so uptight about doing everything just right. I figured that if I could learn to tie my own shoelaces and brush my own teeth, I might be able to learn how to talk the "Marylyn way." I concentrated on doing two things: listening carefully when she talked, and telling her whatever I was thinking and feeling. What a difference this made!

These days, Marylyn can't wait for me to get home from work. She sets me down, she brings me something to drink, and we start talking as if we'd been doing it since kindergarten. She tells me her deepest thoughts and feelings and secrets, and I focus on what she says. Then I tell her mine. I don't do anything exceptional, but she thinks I'm the greatest guy in the world.

Let me give you another example of how a lighter approach has helped my marriage. Marylyn likes romance, and during our courtship and early years of marriage, we had lots of it. It came naturally then. We spent countless hours cuddling, gazing into each other's eyes, and dreaming of the blissful life we would share together. But then, like most couples, we became consumed by the realities of life—crying children, mortgage payments, household projects, and career hurdles to jump. Romance waned, and so did Marylyn's marital satisfaction.

She would gently point out her need for more romance, and I would commit myself to meeting this need. But I felt pressure to be the Perfect Lover. It was as if I thought I had to strum a guitar while humming a love song with a rose between my teeth. I was sure I had to send dozens of flowers, compose sonnets to recite from below her bedroom window, and tango gracefully across a dance floor with her in my arms. My expectations for myself were so high and unreasonable that I usually ended up doing nothing.

Then one day I realized I needed to lighten up, to stop putting so much pressure on myself to be the epitome of romance. Now I do a bunch of ordinary things every week that are easy and enjoyable for me and that spark romance for Marylyn. I sometimes buy her a book I know she'll like, and I write little poems about my love for her on the first page. She goes crazy over them! I call her in the middle of the day and tell her I'm thinking of her. She eats that up too.

Other times, I take Marylyn to the beach in the evening. We leave our shoes and socks in the car, and we stroll on the wet sand in our bare feet. I hold her hand, wax poetic about the sunset, mention some faraway places I'd love to take her, and she's like putty in my hands. Then if I buy her an ice-cream cone, spread a blanket out on the beach, and ask her about her dreams for the future, she's all over me. Now I wonder, *What was I so worked up about before? This romance stuff is a cinch!*

Marital Synchrony and the Lighter Touch

Swing easy! It all starts with an assumption that when you and the love of your life get synchronized, your marriage will have a maximal chance for happiness and fulfillment. Let your relationship develop its own rhythm, and your life together will be full of stimulation and excitement. All the meaning and purpose for which the two of you have eagerly searched will suddenly appear. Trying too hard will become a well-intentioned relic of your distant past. Swinging easy will become your effective new strategy.

The kind of synchrony we're talking about comes from unexpected places. Hard work is seldom one of those places. Laughter almost always is. Shared emotional moments are another. Inspirational experiences of many kinds blend us at deep levels. Hopefulness, productive conflict resolution, an ever-present sense of trust in your partner—all of these are fountainheads from which synchrony flows.

Not long ago, Marylyn and I walked together through a difficult experience, and an unexpected source of marital synchrony both challenged and graced our marriage. We were stunned to our depths to learn that my partner of twenty-five years, Dr. Paul Victor Roberts, had died. He was only fifty-six years old. Dr. Roberts was a premier psychologist, but more important, he was the kindest and sweetest man I've ever met. Although he and I had practiced in separate locations for five years, we shared thousands of experiences that built a deep bond between us. I dearly loved this man, and I always will.

I must admit that when I was asked to deliver one of the tributes at his funeral, I was honored but also concerned that I might not be able to contain my emotions.

Marylyn helped me write my tribute to this man we often referred to as Saint Paul. Then she and I worked on my delivery, and she helped me gain control over my feelings and my expression of them. I became more confident that I would be able to hold myself together.

Finally, the day of the funeral arrived, and Marylyn sat next to me in the front row of the church. There would be at least thirty minutes of songs and prayers before I was to speak, and Marylyn repeatedly squeezed my arm to let me know she was supporting me and pulling for me—and praying for my emotional strength.

At last, my time came. I walked forward to the microphone and faced the overflow crowd. I began with as strong a voice as I could. I had memorized every word, and though I have spoken dozens of times in front of large audiences, I spoke words in those four minutes with more feeling than any I have ever spoken. When I finished, I took my seat beside Marylyn. We carefully avoided eye contact because we were brimming with emotion, but she again squeezed my arm to let me know she was proud of me.

Marylyn and I held our emotions in check until the end of that magnificent service. But after the benediction when the organist played "O Canada," the anthem we so often heard Paul sing with the passion of a native son, I sat down on a bench and sobbed. All my emotions let loose, and when I looked at Marylyn, she was crying as well.

As we walked outside into the dark night, Marylyn and I held on to each other—like two people who had just been resynchronized by a powerful shared experience.

Marital synchrony comes from a thousand natural sources. In my opinion, this one had most to do with our common love for our friend Paul Roberts. But just as important was Marylyn's natural way of being there for me: her sensitivity to my plight, her bolstering of my strength, her congratulations for my composed performance, and her blending of her pain with my own. Who would have thought that a funeral would have contributed so potently to the growth of our love? Clearly, our shared experience was crucial. From one perspective, we were unknowingly strengthening our marriage, but it all seemed genuine and gentle.

Marital growth almost always develops this way. When you watch for them, unexpected and uncontrived sources of marital synchrony multiply the richness of your relationship.

The Seed of Love: Feeling Good About Myself in Your Presence

It is obvious to me from my practice of psychology that my love for another person is strongly related to my love for myself when we are together. If the most potent motivation in my life is to feel good about myself—and I believe it is—then I will love an individual most when she helps me to feel best about myself.

You can employ all kinds of strategies to maximize the likelihood that another person will feel good about himself when you're together. You can laugh, tell the person the things you especially like about him, or work hard to meet the needs you detect. All of these strategies may work at one time or another. But I want to tell you about a strategy that works nearly every time.

There is something at the center of your being called *consciousness*. If I ask you about what you are thinking and feeling at this very moment, your answer will emerge from a careful analysis of your most recent consciousness.

Here's my point: love tends to result when your partner is at the center of your consciousness, especially when you are in each other's presence. There is something about my knowing that Marylyn's thoughts and feelings are focused on me that assures me of my importance to her. My importance to her makes me feel good about myself. When we are together and our consciousness is centered on each other, our love is bound to grow steadily and consistently.

This is a central point for dozens of matters about love that we will explore in this book. I call this principle *focus of consciousness*, and I think it is fundamental to the love process.

Consider again my funeral experience. As we sat on the front row of that crowded church, Marylyn repeatedly communicated my place at the center of her consciousness by squeezing my arm. I knew exactly what each squeeze meant: "I am right here with you. I am pulling for you every moment. I am feeling your fear, but I am praying for you. We are in this together. I know how eager you are to honor your dear friend, not to lose control of your emotions, and I am sure you will do well."

These thoughts generate powerful love feelings. When Marylyn and I are in the center of each other's consciousness, our love deepens like the roots of a mighty redwood.

Merged Experience and Focused Consciousness

The secret to cultivating love is maximizing the number of life experiences in which you and your partner are deeply captured by a momentary or lasting event. When I say "deeply captured," I mean that the event exists right at the center of your thoughts and feelings. If *both* of you are focused on one experience, and if your focus of consciousness includes both the event and your partner, the power of this moment to stimulate love between you will be maximal.

Let's say that you and the love of your life have a keen appreciation of music. You are visiting Boston, as Marylyn and I did recently, and you walk across town from your hotel to Symphony Hall. It's a cold winter night, and you are bundled up in warm clothes complete with scarves and gloves. You hold each other tightly as you walk briskly through the frigid air. You are excitedly chatting as you stride along, but your tongues are thick and your lips are nearly frozen.

When you arrive, you duck inside and feel the welcome warmth. As you check your coats and your gloves, you chuckle together at how wonderful the heated hall is after being out in the frosty air. You hand your tickets to the usher, and you are led to perfect seats. You chat about the brilliance of your concierge. You read the program and point out little details to each other.

Then the conductor appears, and the crowd hushes. The orchestral sounds send chills down your spines. You reach out for the other's hand, and you grasp tightly. The music takes you straight up for a while, and then it lets you float. It flies you through the air like a glider on a still day, and the two of you love the ride. Soon, the music grows softer and softer, and it carries you through some low places—and then more low places. Your hands lose their vibrant feel. But finally, the music soars again, and you have a thousand thoughts and feelings about what it is saying and how it moves you.

This is what I mean by a shared experience. The more

of these you have, especially the ones when you are holding on to each other and feeling each other's heart beating, the more you will bond with the deepest parts of each other's life. Your consciousness is merged, your experience together is blended, and your lives are becoming one. You are not exactly making it happen, but it is happening to the two of you simultaneously.

Making Your Marriage a Symphony

This book is all about two ideas that have become sacred to me. The first is that marriage can become a magnificent symphonic experience. You and your spouse may play different instruments, but you play in partnership with each other. Your eventual performance will be a thousand times better than anything one of you could have produced alone. Often, both of you will contribute to a mighty crescendo, a sudden sorrowful passage, or a delightful flight through the galaxy. One of you may lead and the other follow, and then you change positions. Other times you listen to each other while one of you is playing a passage alone, maybe for a long interval. But whatever the details, this is your project, your symphony, and you are committed to making it extraordinary for both partners.

My second idea is that the most beautiful music you make comes from within you, virtually without work. The single most likely source of this "music" will be experiences you and your spouse share, experiences in which you feel each other's deepest and most passionate support. The goal of your living will be the growth of your love and the maximizing of your mutual joy. Through all the ups and downs of life, you will try to keep your lover's interest at the center of your consciousness, and you will know that when this happens, sublime joy and happiness will be yours. You will be sharing in the experience of love, sharing so fully and so deeply that you will come closer to the heart of God than you ever thought possible.

2

Fan the Flames
of Romance

Imagine this scenario: it's December, two weeks before Christmas, and you and the love of your life are spending the weekend at a cozy mountain cabin. Mounds of freshly fallen snow blanket the ground outside, and the wind is howling. It's cold, between ten and twenty degrees, but you have a fire crackling in the fireplace and plenty of extra wood. Your favorite music is playing softly, and there are several more delightful CDs queued up. The two of you have been skiing all day, and now that you've stowed your equipment and changed into comfortable clothes, the evening stretches out in front of you.

Standing in front of the fire, you glance at this person who is wondrously special to you. You smile at each other and move close. You embrace tightly and sway to the music. You slowly move around the room together. You kiss each other lightly. The words lingering in your mind are, *This is so romantic.*

What Does "This Is So Romantic" Mean?

I've seldom met a husband and wife who don't hunger for more romance. An extra dose of ardor and affection can heal a hundred hurts and spark new hope for two worn-out lovers. Renewed romance weaves you together again, soul to soul. It reminds you of why you fell in love in the first place. It puts you back in touch with each other's best qualities.

Certain relational dynamics are almost always present during romantic moments. The scene I described contains many of them. First, there is the dynamic of safety. You are shielded from the enemies of romance—the myriad factors that thwart intimacy in everyday life. You are away from crying babies and clamoring children. There is no stack of bills to be paid, no E-mail to check, no ringing phone demanding your attention. Your romantic moments are protected from interruptions and invasions.

The mountain cabin scene also has the dynamic of sensuality woven into it. There is something inviting about the sound and smell of a crackling fire, especially in contrast to the howling wind and snowy cold outside. And soft music evokes dozens of warm feelings, many of them from shared memories. You are happily tired from the skiing; your muscles are relaxed from the enjoyable exercise. You hold each other and feel each other's soft skin. You move around the room in rhythm to the music. This is indeed sensual!

This romantic interlude may contain nostalgia, which often contributes to passionate feelings. Maybe you and your partner have been to this cabin before, and you are reminded of other experiences that kindled your love. Perhaps the stereo is playing "your" song, the one that was featured at your wedding reception or the one on the radio when you first kissed.

You and your partner are away, maybe far away, from the mundane. You feel extremely special to each other. You are secure and warm. You are able to concentrate on your individual and collective needs. Your love, always assumed to be present, has moved to the forefront of your consciousness.

This is *so* romantic.

We Need a Romance Gauge on the Marital Dashboard

It's a fact of life that marriages get bogged down with routine duties and regular responsibilities. We work hard to make a living, raise our kids the best we know how, keep ourselves reasonably clean and organized, and attend to the mail and phone calls and never-ending birthdays and holidays. Sometimes we forget about marriage's desperate need for romance. We assume that somehow our love will endure without much attention.

Then, for whatever reason, the marital "symptoms" begin to pile up. We often fail to recognize them for what they are—warning lights on the marital dashboard signaling a need for action. Day after day, week after week, we continue getting up in the morning, going about our business, and retiring to sleep at night, all the while failing to notice the red "check engine" light staring us in the face.

The intensity of marital conflict increases, and our times of feeling distant become more frequent. It may have been a long time since we scheduled a romantic weekend, but we don't think about what we are missing or the cost of our inattention. We are occupied with what we *think* is important, and we ignore what is *really* important.

What an Impact Romance Makes in the Lives of the "Romanced"

There is an old story about romance, variations of which I have heard for years. It involves a man who no longer found his wife attractive. She was caustic, dour, overweight, and frumpy. The two of them were virtually at war, and they possessed not a shred of marital happiness. The man eventually decided to divorce his wife, and he wanted the divorce to really hurt her, so he consulted a divorce attorney.

The attorney listened to all the man's venomous and

vengeful words, then he offered some advice. "Here's what I want you to do," he said to the husband. "Go home and spend the next thirty days treating your wife like the most important person in the world. Engage her in conversation and listen attentively. Help around the house. Take her to dinner, and see a romantic movie with her once a week. Call her a couple of times each day, and send her an unexpected gift once or twice during the month. Do everything in your power to be kind to her. And then you will have her set up for the biggest hurt of her life! When you walk away from her, she will be devastated. I'll have the divorce papers ready in exactly thirty days."

The husband thought about the advice and concluded that it might work. His wife wouldn't expect such behavior, and if he pulled it off, it might provide the vicious touch he had been looking for. He went home and immediately put into practice all the unscrupulous suggestions the attorney had given him.

On the twenty-seventh day, the attorney called to make final arrangements for serving the divorce papers. But the husband became horrified at the very suggestion of divorce.

"Divorce?" he said. "Why in the world would I want to divorce her? She's an incredible woman, even better than when we first fell in love. She is everything I've dreamed of since my youth. I wouldn't divorce her for the world!"

However corny this story may be, it makes a point I have witnessed dozens of times in my psychotherapy practice. When one partner begins treating the other romantically, everything shifts and changes in the relationship. There is something about being treated in this special way that makes you want to reciprocate. Fortunately or unfortunately, new romantic efforts often get started only when marital pain reaches the I-can't-take-it-anymore level. This becomes the point at which a critical decision must be made: either end the marriage or pursue more romance.

Romance Should Involve Your Deepest Needs

As I said earlier, the primary motivation in life for all of us is to feel good about ourselves. And the person you marry is almost always in the best position to help you feel this way. Why? Because you let this person know you at the deepest levels. Because of your spouse's commitment to you, the undying pledge of lifelong love, you take one emotional risk after another with him or her. Since your spouse knows you so well, his or her feelings about you are monumentally important. If your spouse likes you, you feel liked at a fundamental level of your being.

Romance is all about relating to each other in such a way that your primary, mutual importance becomes obvious enough for each of you to hear—to hear and dare to experience.

I have concluded that romance is not really romance until your relating with each other starts to involve your deepest individual needs. If these needs revolve around the question of whether you can individually feel good about yourself, then you can begin to understand why romance is so vital to each of you. When it becomes painfully and wonderfully apparent that your individual fulfillment is wrapped up with your marital closeness, you will recognize why you must nurture romantic love. If you fail to find the time, your marriage will wither, and your own psychological health may become more and more fragile.

For a thousand different reasons, then, you need regular, frequent experiences of romance. You need to snuggle with your spouse in front of a roaring fire on a snowy night, listen to gorgeous music, linger over a delicious meal, and take the time to know that all is well. Most of all, you desperately need to be assured of your special importance at the center of the other's consciousness. You need to hear those miraculous words whispered again and again, "I love you—and I will for as long as I live." You need to feel attended to without interruption, listened to without preoccupation, held for a long time without the urgency to hurry off somewhere. You need to experience all over again the excitement of becoming one flesh with the person who holds the key to your heart.

The Essence of Romance

Through the years, I have analyzed romance from every conceivable perspective, and I have reached five conclusions on the topic. My goal is to trigger *your* brain so that you will invest more time and energy in developing romance in your marriage.

1. *Romance is all about love, and love is virtually impossible to give until you have learned to love yourself.*

There is something wonderful about my knowing that Marylyn loves me, but in order for me to love richly in return, my self-love needs to be well established deep at the center of myself. And when I get myself loved in this central way, only then am I capable of loving her.

One of the most frustrating dilemmas I face as a psychologist is this: two persons in an unloving relationship come to me because their marriage is dry and in need of romance. The husband or wife will say, usually in a listless, monotone voice, "Our marriage has grown stale. There's no magic, no spark, no passion. It's just the same old, boring routine week after week, month after month. I don't even know why we're together anymore."

My first impulse is to tell them, "The solution is simple. Romance your marriage back to health! Fan the embers of your passion until they burst into flames. Stay at your favorite hotel for the weekend; dine at the restaurant where you had your first date; hold hands as you window-shop downtown; send her flowers; bring him breakfast in bed."

Indeed, many marriages that have hit a dry spell simply need an infusion of romance and passion. But the solution isn't always that simple. Sometimes one or both partners have "internal" work to do. Each individual must develop a loving relationship within himself or herself before he or she will be able to love the other person. In these cases, my task is to help the husband or wife achieve this kind of individual loving relationship.

2. Romance requires that two people demonstrate the high priority each has in the other's life.

There is nothing romantic about being in the same room with another person who is watching a football game on television and ignoring his partner. Equivalently, there is nothing romantic about being in the same house for a whole evening with someone who is continually on the phone. The fundamental secret of romance is the matter of priority. When two people get a strong sense that they matter more to each other than anything else in the world, romance is about to bloom.

I find it fascinating that all of us crave to matter *most* to someone else. It's not good enough to be second in someone's life. Being first makes marital love unique. If you matter most to your spouse, and your spouse matters most to you, all you need is the right place and enough time for romance to flourish.

3. *Focus of consciousness is especially relevant to romance.*

If all the elements are in place for romance, but one person's consciousness is focused on what's happening in a business deal or what's cooking on the stove, the romantic moment loses its power. I need to know *in this moment* that everything in my partner's mind is focused on *me*. If I am not at the center of my partner's immediate thoughts and feelings, and she is not at the center of mine, romance is sure to fizzle or at least to be weak and unsatisfying.

There is one other consideration about this point. If my partner is focused on something else right now, how much can I call her attention back to me and this moment? And what price does this extract from the experience of romance?

For instance, if I'm walking down the street with my partner, holding hands, feeling good, and I suddenly sense that she isn't present, that her mind has moved to some problem, it certainly dampens a romantic moment. I can say to her, "I sense that you're distracted and focused elsewhere. Come on back; I'm dying for us to be totally together this afternoon." But this is a big bucket of water poured over the romantic cinders. Recovery is possible, but for romance to have a great run of moments, both of us must stay very focused on each other—without interruption if at all possible.

Focus of consciousness is a vital part of the love dynamic. It makes a shared experience truly shared. If our minds are somewhere else, our hearts are sure to go to sleep, and when this happens, romance melts like a Popsicle on a blistering hot day.

4. *Romance thrives when all senses are activated.*

If the two of you smell really good to each other, this sure helps romance along. If music you both enjoy plays in the background, that is one more plus. If the stars are bright and the night sky is lit up with all of its magnificent jewelry, that's another contribution. If your partner and you sip a warm, soothing drink that tantalizes your taste buds, that further enhances the experience. And if your partner's hand feels soft like a baby's skin, what a boost to loving feelings. When all of your senses are wide open and alive, romance is almost sure to reach its highest level.

Sometimes the surrounding circumstances are nearly as important as the inner mood. For instance, romance gets crowded out in the middle of a heavy workday, but leisure time creates a wonderful atmosphere for romantic relating. Similarly, high-anxiety situations, ones that draw your attention away from each other, are less likely to produce loving feelings.

When circumstances are right, your senses have a chance to infiltrate your consciousness. All of a sudden you have time to smell fragrant flowers, hear birds singing, and view a beautiful vista. More important, you have a greater chance of concentrating your sight, touch, and the rest of your senses on the person you love the most.

5. *Romance must involve both partners.*

Perhaps nothing in the world is more frustrating than being in a one-way romantic relationship. One unromantic partner can create such a drag on any relationship that the marital romance level will keep sinking lower and lower until it disappears. But I will tell you this: I've watched many individuals keep working with their partners until finally the spark of romance ignites into a passionate flame.

Several years ago, I counseled a physician and his wife whose marriage had an acute case of the blahs. The wife was dreamy and romantic, and she was dying for her husband to reciprocate. But he was a busy man who saw patients all day and frequently took emergency calls at night. He got up before daylight and worked until well after dark. By the time he got home, he was physically and emotionally drained. When his wife cried out for a little romance, he had no energy, no ability to focus his consciousness on her.

Fortunately, this persistent woman didn't give up. She genuinely loved her husband, and she was convinced that he genuinely loved her too (though he certainly didn't offer much evidence of this initially). She packed lunches for him and included love notes. She sometimes got up before he did—early—and fixed his favorite breakfast. And occasionally, she colluded with his office manager to clear his schedule on a Friday afternoon, and she whisked him away for a long weekend at a beach cottage. She went after him with a loving heart and fierce determination.

Only the most coldhearted man wouldn't respond to such thoughtful treatment, and I'm happy to say this doctor's romantic spirit was resuscitated. In time, he started enjoying their romantic moments so much that he took the initiative to plan dates and getaways.

As the wife told me at our final session, "Let's face it. Romance requires two fully engaged participants. When I was the only one pursuing romance, I felt like I was making huge investments without any returns. But I knew I would one day reap the dividends—and I have. Our marriage has never been better . . . or more passionate."

For his part, the husband said, "I can't believe I overlooked this beautiful woman for so long." Then he added with a grin, "I guess I'll just have to make up for lost time."

It does happen! If your love life is currently one-sided, don't give up. With enough wooing and nurturing, even the most faintly glowing ember can be rekindled into a roaring blaze.

How to Make Romance Come Alive in Your Marriage

There is every reason to expect that your romance rating can and will soar to new heights. If the two of you simply want it to, it stands a great chance of happening. And when it does, everything about your relationship will become more exciting to both of you. The prize for positive change in your level of romance is definitely worth any work required of you.

Having said that, I hasten to add that you should be optimistic *and* realistic. Look for progress, not miracles. What I mean is that a 10 percent yearly growth rate is definitely attainable, and if you will set your sights at this level, you are likely to experience one year after another of romantic revitalization. Five years from now, your marriage can be significantly more romantic.

With those foundational points made, let's look at specifics. What follows is a seven-point romance-rejuvenation program.

1. *As obvious as it sounds, you and your partner need to spend time together.*

I mean ample, consistent time together. Some couples hardly see each other throughout the week and then expect their romance to rekindle immediately on Saturday night. But it's tough to pick up where you left off if there's no ongoing communication and check-in time.

Marylyn and I are together virtually every evening. We both work outside the home, and we finish our workdays at six o'clock. Since we drive two cars, we usually talk in the late afternoon and make our evening plans. Sometimes we meet at a local restaurant, and sometimes we're both eager to get home. One way or another, we almost always spend the evening together, and I can't tell you how much our marital romance profits from the "everydayness" of our contacts.

Over dinner, we catch up on the day's events. We talk about the people we saw, the tasks we accomplished, the things that went well, and the things that went wrong. Whenever possible, we move beyond reporting on the day to discussing how we felt and responded to what transpired. I look forward to this unwinding far more than I look forward to eating dinner.

This daily ritual keeps each of us woven into the other's life. Each of us knows most of the details of what the other faces every day and genuinely cares about the progress of the other's life. It helps us know each other from the center of our souls to the outer edges of our interests. It's not so much that we talk for a long time about our days; it's that we take a huge interest in each other, and these nightly catch-ups are like reading newspaper accounts of our favorite teams.

2. Dream together.

Dreams involve goals and objectives for your individual lives and for your marriage. A great dream for your marriage needs to be a great dream for her, a great dream for him, and a great dream for the two of you. These marital dreams help you most when you keep them current. If they grow out of date, they inevitably lose their power to motivate and inspire you.

I encourage you to have a dream for the next year of your marriage, another for the next five years, and still another for the next ten years. And I encourage you to work on your dreams at least twice a year—perhaps on your anniversary and the six-month point.

Dreaming together and working toward the realization of the shared dream contribute dramatically to the level of romance in your marriage.

(For more information and ideas about dreaming together, read my book *Learning to Live with the Love of Your Life . . . and Loving It.*)

3. Take time every day to consciously pull for each other.

If prayer is natural for you, spend plenty of time praying for your mate. I have become a passionate believer in prayer, and I spend time nearly every day praying for Marylyn. I am convinced that her life is substantially more meaningful because of these prayers.

But the positive effects from prayer go significantly further. They greatly affect our love for each other. It comes back to the focus-of-consciousness concept. When you pray for your partner, he or she is right at the center of your consciousness. All your hopes and best wishes are focused on that person as you ask God to intervene in his or her life.

4. Schedule a time with your spouse at least once a month.

It doesn't really matter what you do during your time together as long as you both find it enjoyable. You can drive together to a remote area that you love, explore an old ghost town, browse in your favorite bookstore, take a picnic lunch to the park, or visit an art museum.

Whatever you do on this day, the time away will meet your marital need for romance as little else can. It will offer the promise of time to catch up, time to rekindle your flame of love for each other, and time to recommit yourselves to the "one life" that excited you so much when you got married. You will begin to anticipate these times, and half the fun will be planning them.

5. *At least twice a year, get away with your lover for an extended period of time.*

As enriching as short outings are, you also need unhurried, relaxing days to nurture your love. If at all possible, go to a place that is beautiful, one that is conducive to letting go of tension and daily concerns.

I began this chapter with an example of such a weekend in the mountains. But there are plenty of options for weekend getaways. Many couples find that being near water is conducive to romance. Travel to the ocean for the weekend or to a favorite lake or river.

You don't need to break your budget to spend extended time away. Find a little cabin, pack up the camping gear, or borrow a camper from your friend or parents. Whatever you decide, do it! And when you do, make sure that times of romance are central to your daily schedule. That means walks along the water in the morning, long naps in the afternoon, moonlit dinners and dancing and cuddling under the stars in the evening.

6. *Find a way both of you can serve others.*

Years ago, I read a research study indicating that persons who care for others together tend to develop respect, appreciation, and attraction for each other. We need to take better advantage of this simple, but meaningful, way of growing the romantic side of the marital relationship.

Caring for others makes us feel good about ourselves. Don't forget this principle: we are most attracted to those people in whose presence we feel best about ourselves. One way to feel good about yourself is to help other persons who need what you have to offer. When you and your spouse serve together and feel great about it, all kinds of positive, loving feelings are bound to follow.

7. *Regularly remind each other of your mutual significance to each other.*

Look for every opportunity to communicate to your spouse, "You are the most important person in my life." You can convey this through spoken or written words or through acts of kindness. I told you earlier how I sometimes buy Marylyn a book and include a little poem in the front. Other times I bring her a Mounds candy bar, her favorite. She could certainly buy herself a book or a Mounds bar. That's not the point! These small gestures assure her that she is at the center of my consciousness, which draws her closer to me.

There you have it! This seven-step approach to enhancing your marital romance will definitely work.

Begin right now to put it into practice, and I guarantee that you will love the results.

Marital Romance Is a Brilliant Investment

I'd like to spend much more time talking about romance, but I've got to go now. Marylyn and I have a date to see a movie this afternoon. Both of us have been wanting to see Tom Hanks's new film, and it starts at 4:40 P.M. You can bet I will practice what I've preached to you in this chapter. I'll sit as close as I can to Marylyn during the show, take her out to eat afterward, ask her a thousand questions about how she felt about this and that, listen to her every word with great care, and let her know that she is far and away the dearest person in my life. Maybe you would like to take your lover on a date this afternoon too.

Here is the last thing I want to say before I leave for my rendezvous: if you decide to, you can make your marriage more and more romantic for the rest of your days together. And I know from personal experience that every investment you make in the growth of your romantic relationship will pay greater dividends than any other investment you can ever make.

Be courageous. Take the first step in letting your partner know how special he or she is to you. Be persistent too. There is nothing you can do for your marriage that will mean half as much as your diligent efforts to show your partner how much you care. Finally, be optimistic. Your romance *will* grow, and when it does, your marriage will be significantly more fulfilling.

3

Refuel Your Relationship with Laughter and Levity

Last night, Marylyn and I arrived home after work feeling tired, grumpy, and irritable. We had gotten up early in the morning, put in a long workday, and dealt with several problems and crises. Sorting through the mail—bills and advertisements—didn't do anything to lift our spirits. Neither did the phone call—a solicitation for mortgage insurance—that came as we prepared a simple dinner.

As we sat down to eat, I sensed it was one of those nights that could quickly sink into a morass of gloom. It was also the kind of night in which our crankiness was barely veiled and could easily rear its ugly head. I decided to try something.

"Do you know what I thought about today?" I said.

Marylyn said, "Uh-uh," as she buttered a roll.

"I don't know why this memory came to me, but I thought about the Nassau Inn," I replied with a little smirk. "You know what I'm talking about."

A smile formed on her face. "Of course I do."

That was all we needed to get us going, and we spent the next ten minutes reliving an incident that has become part of our family lore. It occurred years ago in Princeton, New Jersey, when our three daughters were young. We had made a nostalgic return to the town that had meant so much to us when we were in graduate school at Princeton Seminary. We loved to eat at the Nassau Inn, a formal, extravagant restaurant that had fabulous food. We forgot it was a place for stodgy old fogies who wanted nothing to do with children until they were in their early forties. Nevertheless, we were ushered to a table for five, complete with a linen tablecloth, crystal goblets, and a lineup of silverware that seemed impossible to use during one meal.

Soon after we were seated, Lindsay, our youngest, began to cry, and every eye in the room locked onto us. We tried to distract her by offering her everything in Marylyn's purse and my pockets, but she was negotiating for a lot more (maybe our combined inheritances). With a red face, Marylyn picked up the now-shrieking little girl and headed for the ladies' room. In the process, Luann, our middle child, dropped her knife on the floor and dived under the table to retrieve it. As I leaned over to tell her to get off the floor, I spotted five-year-old Lorrie reaching for a big glass of ice water.

"No!" I nearly shouted as I grabbed the glass, spilling half the contents.

My raised voice and sudden movement startled Lorrie, and she began to cry—one of those cries that starts with a faint whimper and crescendos into a full-throttled wail. It was kind of like a fire engine's siren that begins in the distance and grows louder and louder until it assaults your eardrums.

All the while, Luann was rummaging around for her knife on the floor, where she discovered other valuable treasures ("Look, Dad! I found a penny and a mint!").

I asked her to "get up from there!" in one of those clenched-jaw tones that overshoots the intended volume and can be heard by everyone within twenty feet.

Lorrie, now choking back tears, went after the water again. I could still hear Lindsay blubbering in the rest room.

An elderly couple, stuffy looking in their starched formalwear, pointedly cleared their throats while glaring at me. A waiter appeared and asked if he could be of service. I asked if he had any baby-sitting experience, which he didn't find amusing. After another five minutes of this hubbub, we got the kids calm enough to wolf down a hurried meal before another eruption could take place.

I assure you, this embarrassing episode was not the least bit amusing at the time. But over the years, it has evolved into one of our family stories that gets funnier and funnier the more we tell it. And as Marylyn and I took turns filling in details last night, our gloom turned to gaiety. We ended up laughing uproariously, and we thoroughly enjoyed the rest of the evening as we recalled one hilarious memory after another.

Humor, Laughter, and the Lighter Touch

When two people want to strengthen their marriage, they can travel several different paths to achieve that goal. The path I recommend is paved with humor, levity, and lightheartedness. I use these "tools" in my marriage, and I encourage every husband and wife to do the same.

In my psychotherapy practice, I regularly counsel couples who are frustrated with their conflicts and problems. My job is to shed light, to help each understand the other better, forgive each other, and work through their difficulties. I have a choice about how to perform my role. I can delve into the problems and grapple with the conflicts, or I can move in a more positive direction. The truth is that both functions are crucial to the eventual reconstruction of the marriage. But I now believe that my former approach—to work my head off to help them resolve the conflicts—was a gross exaggeration of that alternative's potential for bringing help. I now emphasize this lighter and more delightful approach.

Marital humor is key to this effort. It becomes both a

social lubricant and a vital contributor to the marital revitalization effort. Its value soars as two people have shared experiences, as they include each other in these experiences, and as they perceive their togetherness in the center of this experiencing. Then, it seems to me, their laughter produces the sealing bond that brings them together in ever more meaningful ways.

Laughter Is Fuel in a Couple's Gas Tank

Tim and Jennifer approached me after one of my marriage seminars. Parents of two boys under six, they were "overworked, underpaid, and exhausted all the time."

"We need help getting our marriage back on track," Jennifer told me. "We had a happy marriage for the five years before our kids came along, but then . . ." Her voice trailed off, so Tim finished her sentence.

"But then we started fighting, we grew more distant from each other, and our good feelings about our marriage have all but disappeared," he said. "Now we're more like roommates or business partners than spouses."

They asked to make an appointment with me for marriage therapy, and I reluctantly agreed—reluctantly because I wasn't sure that they needed therapy. I know from experience that a couple with small children often need more sleep, more romance, more opportunities to talk, and more time to invest in the relationship. But I told them I'd be happy to help if I could, and we scheduled an appointment for the following week.

When Tim and Jennifer arrived at my office, I asked them to tell me about their relationship in more detail, and they described a scenario I've heard dozens of times.

"I started my own graphic design company last year," Tim said, "and I put in long hours trying to make it go. I come home tired and discouraged—and Jennifer meets me at the door with the boys in tow, ready for me to take over. I need a break, and I'd like some time to tell Jennifer about my day, but I don't get either."

Jennifer was eager to give her side of the story.

"It's not like I go off to the spa or sit and read a magazine when Tim comes home," she said. "When he watches the boys, I do all the household chores I can't get done while chasing two squirmy kids around the house all day. I spend all evening washing dishes, folding laundry, picking up toys."

It was obvious that the beleaguered pair were simply out of fuel. Tim worked too many hours, Jennifer felt neglected, Tim felt unappreciated for his sacrificial labor, and the children were too much for Jennifer to handle by herself. The drain on their energy supply had them perilously close to the marital throw-in-the-towel stage.

Fortunately, both of them were emotionally healthy,

they knew how to communicate, and they wanted their marriage to succeed. They hadn't put any gas in their tank for far too long, so their sputtering and lurching down the freeway of life were totally understandable.

I said to Jennifer, "What do you like most about Tim?"

She didn't want to answer that question. She was frustrated with him, tired of feeling abandoned, fearful that if she said something positive, she would be "letting him off the hook." She sat and stared at the floor, refusing to say anything.

Since I had a pretty good idea of what was going through her mind, I waited.

After about ninety seconds, she looked up at me with a mixture of boredom and disdain on her face. These were her exact words: "I can't remember your question."

"What do you like most about Tim?" I repeated.

After another twenty seconds, she got up the courage to play along.

"His sense of humor, I guess," she said in a low voice.

"Tell me about his sense of humor," I said with a little smile on my face.

"Well," Jennifer began slowly, "Tim is incredibly funny. He doesn't seem to try to be—he just is. And when he gets started, he can keep me laughing for hours."

Bingo! We had turned the corner. I imagined they had talked for months, even years, about all of their problems, but it had probably been forever since they had focused on their good feelings for each other.

Naturally, I asked Tim what he liked best about Jennifer. After all the warning he had received, his answer came instantly: "Jennifer can be the most loving person in the world."

I heard the "can be," but we would come back to his answer later. I was eager to delve into Jennifer's comment about Tim's sense of humor. Why? Because I was looking for some fuel for this relationship, and nothing provides better fuel than humor, laughter, and lightheartedness.

"Let's start with Tim's sense of humor," I said. "Jennifer, give me an example of how he makes you laugh."

She folded her arms across her chest and said, "Well, first I should tell you that he hasn't been funny for months."

"Go back as far as you need to," I told her.

She thought for a while and began with a faint grin on her face. "Well, Tim used to pretend he was a rich guy. In reality, we've always lived from paycheck to paycheck. But one day a couple of years ago, he called me from work and said he wanted to take me out on the town. I asked him what that meant, but he told me to get a baby-sitter and get dressed up, and he would pick me up at six-thirty. I got the kids taken care of, I put on my best dress, and the doorbell rang at exactly six-thirty. Tim had talked one of his friends into driving the company limousine, and the two of them, all decked out in black tie and top hats, were waiting for me. When I answered the door, he said: 'Good evening, Mrs. Jenkins, I am honored that you are able to join me.' I cracked up, but he was totally deadpan. From that moment until we arrived home, I laughed until I cried. It was one of the best times of my life."

While Jennifer was talking, I watched Tim out of the corner of my eye. He was looking away, smiling sheepishly yet proudly. He clearly loved hearing her tell that story. Over the next ten minutes, she relived one detail after another about *the* date when Tim was hilariously funny and, for that night at least, stole her heart away. We all laughed with gusto. Moreover, together we emphasized a different side of their relationship, and we refueled their tanks for the journey toward the revitalization of their marriage.

To be sure, they had plenty of work to do and issues to resolve. But by infusing their relationship with much-needed levity, we created an optimistic attitude that fostered progress.

Why Is Humor So Helpful to a Relationship?

When two people share ten minutes of laughter together, as Tim and Jennifer did, it is powerful medicine for their relationship. Let me tell you why I think laughter is so healing for couples.

It all comes back to a shared experience. We laugh together because we share a humorous view of life. More precisely, we discover that we have interpreted an event or situation in the same way, and because humor is involved, there is something pleasant—and perhaps unusual—about our interpretation. The energizing aspect of laughter in marriage is another example of the idea we discussed earlier; it represents the focus of consciousness. When consciousness is focused on an event that involves both you and your partner, there is a binding together of the two of you at that moment—a binding similar to what occurs when you watch a beautiful sunset together and marvel at its beauty.

Consider why Jennifer found Tim's humor so enjoyable. Tim was a person of average means pretending to be rich. This is what we call incongruous humor. Then he extended the humor by speaking a formal sentence in a formal voice: "Good evening, Mrs. Jenkins, I am honored that you are able to join me." He furthered the incongruity by remaining "deadpan" throughout the evening. Tim's ability to maintain a straight face, while all the time Jennifer knew that he was fully aware of the incongruity, contributed immensely to her enjoyment.

We should look at one other aspect that contributed to Jennifer's statement that "it was one of the best times of my life." Everything about the evening was positive in relation to Tim and Jennifer. He picked her up in a beautiful car, treated her to a fancy dinner, and lavished her with attention and compliments. Jennifer felt that Tim really loved her—that he was both funny and caring. She could not miss how thoroughly he had prepared every detail, and it was obvious to her that his preparation was motivated by his love for her.

Humor in a marriage needs to make both people laugh. If Tim had set up an experience that was in any way demeaning of Jennifer, but humor was involved, marital bonding probably would not have occurred. Some forms of humor, such as sarcasm and mimicry, can be hurtful, even if they are funny. But humor that engages both people in deep-down belly laughter can make a tremendously positive difference in a marriage.

When It Comes to Marriage, Kevin Leman Is America's Funniest Speaker

Marylyn and I have had the pleasure over the past year of being a part of marriage seminars presented in large cities across America. There are five speakers, and we listen to these speakers at every seminar as though we had never heard them before. That's how good they are!

The funniest speaker by far is Kevin Leman, a psychologist

who was for many years the dean of students at the University of Arizona. He has written ten good (and funny) books, but his genius shines most brightly on a stage in front of hundreds or thousands of married couples.

Over the forty-five minutes that Kevin speaks, he has couples bellowing with laughter. He talks in great detail about the differences between men and women, and he nails those differences with such precision that every comment generates more laughter than the one before. When he finishes, the giant audiences stand and clap and whistle their appreciation for this man, and they would applaud for ten straight minutes if time permitted.

What do the couples like so much about Kevin's presentation? He gives them a powerful shared experience, one that is enormously enjoyable for both the husband and the wife. They sit and laugh together for forty-five minutes. I watch them. They hold hands, they hug and kiss, they elbow each other—and all the time they are doing this, they are laughing heartily.

Kevin says what they need to hear too. He tells them things that assure them they are like other couples: their struggles are normal; their frustrations in being different as men and women are common. Kevin slips in all kinds of values with his humor. He lauds marriage and family. He inspires at the very point that he makes people laugh the hardest.

What Do Couples Most Often Laugh About?

Every couple has a different marital funny bone. Some couples get tickled by puns and wordplay. Others respond to hyperbole, using obvious exaggeration to generate laughs. Still others enjoy physical humor—playing pranks and doing silly impressions.

Whatever the form of humor, some subjects make almost all couples laugh. Perhaps the most popular subject is a couple's kids, which is certainly the case for Marylyn and me. When children are learning to walk, talk, and express feelings, parents often find themselves cracking up together. It may be humor that makes parenting bearable because, as every parent knows, the energy required for being a parent is enormous. Sometimes, the emotional requirements (and the financial ones) of parenthood are almost too much, and laughter serves as a valve to let off steam.

I am an enthusiastic fan of Bill Watterson's comic strip "Calvin and Hobbes," and I remember several wonderful strips that featured the subject of child rearing. One went like this: in the first frame, Calvin's mother is looking over a bill, and she is reading it to Calvin's dad: "So the contractor says it will cost $200 to fix."

Calvin's dad has his hand over his eyes as he says, "Oh, that dumb kid!"

In the next frame, Calvin's mom tries to hug Calvin's

dad, who is standing very rigid and leaning away from her. She says, "Well, it's all part of raising a child, right?"

His only reply is "mmm."

Then, with a little smile on her face, the mother says, "You're not sorry we had Calvin, are you?"

His eyes are sort of closed, and he says, "Are YOU?"

In the last frame, the mom has her arms folded, her eyes closed for effect, and she's ready to argue her point: "I asked first . . . Besides, it wasn't all MY decision."

Now Calvin's dad totally loses it. His arms are stretched out to the side, his mouth is wide open, and he says, "All *I* know is that *I* offered to buy us a dachshund, but no, *you* said . . ."

Can you imagine how a conversation like this would eventually lead to squeals of laughter? A few moments later, the couple would probably realize the absurdity of the debate and howl with glee.

I know couples who regularly have funny things happen to them. Marylyn and I have two close friends, Charlene and Claire Johnson, whom we have known for more than thirty years. They are individually endowed with quick wits, and hilarious events seem to follow them as a couple.

On one occasion, Claire became ill, and Charlene drove him to the doctor's office. The male doctor examined Claire in a room that contained a platform elevated a foot above the floor. Having finished his exam, the doctor asked his female nurse to give Claire a shot, and the doctor stepped down and moved over by the door to give Charlene a prescription for Claire.

The nurse told Claire, "Okay, please drop your pants and underwear and bend over."

Claire followed her orders. But just as she plunged the big needle into his backside, the platform gave way, and Claire went sprawling, tripping over his pants. The nurse, trying not to lose control of the needle that was still in Claire, fell on top of him. A loud crash rang out. There lay Claire with his pants around his ankles and the nurse holding on to the needle precariously. Once their safety had been established, Charlene, the doctor, and even the two on the floor could hardly stop laughing. My guess is that the laughter did more healing than the shot.

One of the funniest couples I ever met were Audrey and Roy Kepple, who lived in Kansas City. Roy was my dad's closest friend. The Kepples loved to laugh, and they were great practical jokers. My parents and I visited them for three or four days one time. As we were packing up to leave, Roy said with a straight face, "I hope you're not going to take any of our belongings." We all laughed at the absurdity of his concern.

But when our suitcases were fully packed and carried to the living room, ready to be loaded in the car, Roy announced that he was going to check the guest room just to make sure nothing had been taken. Thirty seconds later, Roy suddenly yelled, "Audrey, Audrey, our blanket is missing—you know, that very expensive one!"

He hurried back to the living room without a trace of a smile. He said to my parents, "I hope you won't take offense, but I must check your bags for stolen goods."

He opened my dad's suitcase, reached down under the clothes, and pulled out the blanket that Roy himself had carefully hidden there. We all laughed uproariously for two or three minutes. The laughter came in waves because Roy, totally deadpan, continued to feign horror and disgust at my dad's "criminal" behavior.

The Humor of Christ

No writing about humor has surprised me more than the scholarly and insightful book by Elton Trueblood titled *The Humor of Christ*. Trueblood argues persuasively that Jesus used humor extensively in His teaching. As a matter of fact, the author maintains that Jesus' humor was crucial to His attractiveness:

> The widespread failure to recognize and to appreciate the humor of Christ is one of the most amazing aspects of the era named for Him. Anyone who reads the Synoptic Gospels with a relative freedom from presuppositions

might be expected to see that Christ laughed, and that He expected others to laugh, but our capacity to miss this aspect of His life is phenomenal. We are so sure that He was always deadly serious that we often twist His words in order to try to make them conform to our preconceived mold. A misguided piety has made us fear that acceptance of His obvious wit and humor would somehow be mildly blasphemous or sacrilegious. Religion, we think, is serious business, and serious business is incompatible with banter.[1]

Trueblood proceeds to point out scores of passages in which Jesus' stories and images seem designed to evoke smiles and even laughter from His audiences. It is now clear to me that Jesus recognized the incredible value of seeing truth from new perspectives. He used irony and satire with precision, and He often skewered the dead-end approaches to life with a rapier wit. He pointed out the way to life's true goals, the ones that involve contentment, meaning, justice, and fairness, and He had people laughing as they both recognized and moved toward those goals.

The Healing Power of a Good Laugh

In the late 1970s, Norman Cousins published his watershed book, *Anatomy of an Illness*. Cousins was well known to most Americans because he had for twenty-five years been the editor of a popular magazine, the *Saturday Review of Literature*. Moreover, he was the author of fifteen highly acclaimed books and had spoken hundreds of times to huge audiences.

In *Anatomy of an Illness,* Cousins chronicled the astounding effects of laughter on his battle against ankylosing spondylitis, a connective tissue disease. In a desperate attempt to get his mind off the pain of the severe inflammation of his spine and joints, he began listening to tapes and watching films that made him laugh uproariously. He discovered that ten minutes of solid belly laughter would give him two hours of pain-free sleep. Cousins's suggestion that laughter could change the course of his illness created an enormous stir in medical circles, and over time, the empirical proof of his claims has been documented repeatedly.

There is no question that laughter contributes significantly to physical health. Researchers have established that persons who value humor most, and who engage in it frequently, are most capable of coping with tensions and ailments. So well recognized are the healing powers of humor and laughter that they are specific parts of treatment for patients in hospitals worldwide.

Here is my extension of this theme: spouses who love to laugh together stand a great chance of overcoming any "ailment" that plagues their marriage. That's because humor is all about perspective. I have noticed that some couples are able to rotate a relational concern so that it amuses them, even though it makes them upset. If they then choose to focus on their amusement, they can sometimes translate a potentially hurtful marital conflict into a laugh-producing event that softens their feelings toward each other.

I once counseled a couple, Jeff and Marianne, who were confronted with a dramatic change in their roles within their marriage. When they married, Jeff was a successful businessman with a considerable financial portfolio. But in a severe downturn of the economy, he lost almost everything. When they came to see me, Jeff had a steady job, but it paid almost nothing.

Marianne had largely based her respect for Jeff on his career achievements and his generosity. Now all that had changed. He was providing less than he was consuming. And he could no longer afford to be as generous as he had been; in fact, he became tightfisted with his meager earnings. To complicate matters, Marianne virtually supported them both with her income. He was depressed, and she was frustrated. He felt like a failure, and she grew tired of his self-pity. Anger lurked just below the surface of every conversation.

Jeff and Marianne struggled through that difficult turn of events—events that could have easily torn them apart.

Despite all their losses, they held on to their sense of humor. Sometimes I would have to be direct and brutally honest with Jeff, and I wondered whether he would get angry or defensive. Fortunately, when the tension became thickest, Jeff was able to shift his perspective and say something witty and trigger free-flowing laughter from the three of us.

He would listen closely to my painfully honest observations, and then he would sit back, close his eyes, lift his head, and say something like: "Boy! It sounds like I've been intent on pulling this marriage down around my sorry head! Some way for me to deal with my business frustration! What kind of a goose am I being?" Then he would make an absurd facial expression to emphasize how ridiculous he had been acting. The more we all laughed, the closer we felt to each other.

Sometimes Jeff would employ self-deprecating humor to defuse a tense moment. He might say, "Wow, I can see how I've been very critical. If I had a nickel for every criticism I've blasted Marianne with, our money worries would be over!" or "People used to tell me I'd make a poor husband, but I didn't think they meant it literally."

With humor as an ally, all the marital dynamics began shifting. His wife would often say something like, "Oh, honey, you sure have been stubborn, but so have I! I have been so disappointed for you and for us. Sometimes I can imagine what a vicious critic I've been." The healing would surge forward.

Perspective is at the heart of humor, and humor is at the heart of healing. A light approach dissolves our defenses and creates the freedom to look at the truth. When we develop a new perspective on old problems, we foster more and more marital happiness.

A Sense of Humor Is a Critical Part of Being Human

I work closely with dozens of couples who are trying to determine whether they should get married. A sense of humor is usually critical to their selection process. For some people, it may be one of the four or five most important qualities they seek.

In one of my books, *How to Know If Someone Is Worth Pursuing in Two Dates or Less,* I encourage single persons to spend time getting to know themselves well. On the basis of their self-knowledge, they are better able to develop a list of their ten most important "must-haves" to guide their search for a soul mate. Nearly every person who completes this exercise recognizes the need to marry someone who can see the funny side of life.

I recently encountered Dostoyevsky's novel *The Adolescent,* which contains this insightful passage:

If you wish to glimpse inside a human soul and get to know a man, don't bother analyzing his ways of being silent, of talking, of weeping, or seeing how much he is moved by noble ideas; you'll get better results if you just watch him laugh. If he laughs well, he's a good man . . . All I claim to know is that laughter is the most reliable gauge of human nature. Look at children, for instance: Children are the only creatures to produce perfect laughter and that's just what makes them so enchanting . . . A laughing and gay child is a sunbeam from paradise to me, a revelation of future bliss when man will finally become as pure and simple-hearted as a babe.[2]

I am convinced that in marriage, two people who laugh frequently together will modify, and sometimes negate, the negative processes that threaten to destroy their relationship. In their laughter, they become as pure and nondefensive as young children.

How Can You Introduce More Humor into Your Marriage?

Let me suggest some ways that you can maximize laughter in your marriage.

First, when you hear a good joke, write it down or

quickly relate it to someone else so you won't forget it. Do you love a good joke as much as I do? I can hardly wait to tell it to Marylyn when I see her at night. She likes to tell me a joke now and then, too, and though she doesn't fancy herself a great joke teller, she clearly enjoys my laughter when she tells one.

Second, look for humorous happenings and statements you can share with your spouse. For instance, in another book by Norman Cousins, *Head First,* he collected notices that appeared in the "Personals" section of the *Saturday Review.* I loved reading some of them to Marylyn. The one that tickled both of us the most was this one:

> Are you no longer able to spring out of bed in the morning the way you used to? Our device, attached to your alarm clock, is adapted from an electric cattle prod and can be readily attached to your bedsprings. Quick morning starts guaranteed. Fast-Riser Service.

Another one made us laugh as well:

> Computer error has resulted in large supply of electric-powered swivel chairs that make approximately 150 high-speed revolutions per minute automatically as soon as body weight hits the seat. Excellent bargain for people who are nausea-resistant.

A third way to introduce more humor into your marriage is to watch funny movies and TV shows. There are dozens of them. One of our favorite films is *Blazing Saddles*. We also erupt together when we watch *The Return of the Pink Panther* and *I Love Lucy* TV episodes.

All kinds of audiocassettes are wonderfully funny as well. Bill Cosby has many of them, and we buy every Garrison Keillor tape that becomes available. A close friend sent us a tape the other day of some radio programs of *Amos and Andy,* and we thoroughly enjoyed them.

Fourth, send each other a funny book now and then. We especially like Erma Bombeck's humor in *The Grass Is Always Greener Over the Septic Tank* and Art Buchwald's *You Can Fool All of the People All of the Time.* And if you want poetry that makes you bellow, try one of Judith Viorst's books, such as *It's Hard to Be Hip Over Thirty and Other Tragedies of Married Life* or *How Did I Get to Be 40 and Other Atrocities.*

Finally, if you and your spouse pray together, don't be afraid to let God in on your marital humor. When Marylyn and I were younger, it would have struck us as sacrilegious to have laughed when we prayed, but no longer. This attitude changed when I was the dean of a graduate school of psychology and we met Agnes Sanford, an incredible woman who wrote many books on prayer, and her equally incredible assistant, Edith Drury. They took it upon themselves to teach Marylyn and me how to pray. The two women had a deeply personal relationship with God that included a wonderful appreciation of humor in His presence. Their insights into God and humor have greatly enriched our marriage. Now, when Marylyn and I pray together, one of us might say, "God, it was hilarious today when the grandkids were here and they . . ." Then we'll crack up over some funny incident. Or "Thank You, God, for the ability to laugh at ourselves. I sure needed it today when I . . ." And again, we'll break out in laughter.

Show me a husband and wife who love to laugh together, and I will show you a couple with an outstanding chance of achieving maximum marital fulfillment. This is a marriage-building resource available to everyone every day. Fill your home with laughter and levity, and your relationship will be refueled regularly.

4

Energize Your Marriage
with Optimism

This is an optimistic chapter about optimistic marriages!

A healthy dose of optimism maximizes marital power and multiplies marital fulfillment. Here's more good news: if you and your partner currently lack this key ingredient, acquiring it is relatively easy.

During the last ten years, dozens of observational and experiential research studies have demonstrated the benefits of optimism in individual lives, in marriages and families, in organizational life, and in society as a whole. These studies show that optimists fare better than pessimists in work, school, and sports. Hopeful, positive people are likely to achieve more goals, handle stress more wisely, overcome depression more quickly, manage disease with far greater effectiveness, and thereby live longer.

If you and the love of your life can learn how to approach your relationship more optimistically, you will surely have a richer marriage, and your risk of marital decay and divorce will be significantly diminished. When the marital challenges become most difficult, shared optimism can make all the difference in your ability to master them.

The Challenge of Remaining Optimistic in Hard Times

At one point in my career, I decided to focus my research and clinical practice on the subject of death and dying. Scores of individuals and couples dealing with loss were referred to me, and I encountered numerous parents whose children had died or were dying. Obviously, the death of a child puts enormous strain on a marriage, and it is not unusual for such a marriage to fall apart. If partners fail to communicate and process their grief together, emotional distance is sure to follow. Then the two spouses try to deal with their sadness as individuals rather than as a couple. In the middle of their anguish and grief, marital bonding can unknowingly but rapidly dissolve. This is a primary reason that many marriages end in divorce after a major family calamity.

Whether or not the marriage breaks apart often hinges on the partners' degrees of optimism. There's a good chance the marriage will survive—and thrive—if they feel hopeful about their ability to coordinate their recovery efforts and draw strength from each other. If they feel pessimistic about their chances of recovery—and their ability to stay united through the process—the marital prognosis will not be good.

I well remember the couple I saw the day after their two children, eight and ten years old, were killed in an automobile accident. I worked with Ken and Sarah for months, and there were times Sarah didn't care about her husband or her marriage. She had no optimism that they could work through their horrible sadness.

During our first several sessions together, Sarah often said something like, "Let's face it. Our entire relationship was built on raising the kids together. Without *them*, there's no future for *us*."

I had guided couples through the ravages of grief many times before, and although I believed Ken and Sarah could make it through together, I knew their marriage was hanging in the balance. My goal was to help them pull together and develop a little optimism about their collective ability to manage their grief. When they were tempted to give up hope and to recklessly act out their sadness and rage, I encouraged them to hang on, to believe that, eventually, solid ground would become available to them on which they could stand. When Sarah talked about wanting to pull out of the marriage, a marriage that seemed agonizingly empty to her without their children, I tried to provide a temporary bridge for them to each other and to a time when they could feel more unified in their partnership.

Obviously, you would like optimism to build up over time, the final result of thousands of experiences in which the partners have proved their collective ability to handle anything they encountered. You would like their marital perspective to have become so positive by the time they encountered an awful family tragedy that their marriage would stand strong in the face of it. But sometimes we have to manufacture a supply of optimism in the midst of a crisis.

I am happy to report that Ken and Sarah stayed optimistic enough to get through the worst days, which in turn gave them the confidence to get through the many less-than-worst days. As time went on, their optimism built, and they handled every last challenge the tragedy unloaded on them. They eventually considered adding to their family, and now they have two more children. Today, their family is strong and resilient again, as is their marriage.

The Radical Difference of an Optimistic Marriage

If your marriage becomes more optimistic, it will happen because the two of you develop confidence in your combined ability to deal with future challenges effectively and harmoniously. Let's say you have three children who want and deserve college educations. With the skyrocketing cost of college these days, this prospect could be daunting! But to the degree that you and your spouse are optimistic, to that same degree you will be secure in your ability to meet the impending financial demands. If you have confidence that somehow the finances will all come together, you're likely to manage the challenge in such a way that increases the chance of success.

Similarly, if your children are moving toward the teenage years, your degree of marital optimism will determine how confident you are that you will be able to handle together the challenges of being good parents to teenagers. And if you and the love of your life are facing retirement together, your optimism will relate to your level of confidence that whatever the problems of advancing age, even if they include physical or mental deterioration, you will be able to handle them.

Here's the critical point: the more optimistic you are as a couple, the more effective you will be in your moments of challenge. Moreover, the more optimistic you are, the more relaxed and peaceful your marriage will be long before problems occur.

If optimism brings effectiveness in life, pessimism contributes equally to ineffectiveness. And if optimism usually results in peacefulness and confidence, pessimism is both a cause and a companion of doubt and depression.

Optimism Can Be Contagious

Christine and Michael first came to see me for counseling before they were married. He was thirty, and she was twenty-four. Both had come from divorced homes, and they wanted to carefully weigh their decision to marry.

It became immediately apparent to me that Christine was having a tough time keeping Michael on the road to marriage. Every time they encountered a new problem, Michael got cold feet, and he started looking for an exit. Christine listened attentively to his doubts and his caution, and then she constructed a case for why they should still pursue marriage.

Michael was open to her influence, but he was determined not to repeat the divorce of his parents, which had caused so much pain for him and his siblings. He tried to evaluate the data Christine presented, data supporting her contention that their marriage could be fulfilling for both of them. But Michael's chronic pessimism caused him to continually focus on their deficits even as he minimized their assets. He was more invested in guarding against failure than in taking any chances to gain a satisfying relationship.

Christine, on the other hand, tended to see every problem as a challenge to be managed, and since her focus was on their strengths as a couple, she believed they would be able to successfully confront any problem. She emphasized their positive potential as a couple while Michael's mind was dominated by his fears and worries.

"Michael, we've taken several premarital tests, and every one shows that we're well matched," Christine would say. "And we've worked through many issues in counseling. Our relationship is great, and there's no reason to think it won't continue being great after we're married."

"Yes, but two people don't really know how they'll do until they're married," Michael would inevitably protest. "Tests, counseling—all that's fine, but I'm sure our parents thought they were well matched when *they* got married. In fact, I'm sure all couples considering marriage think they're going to beat the odds and stay together forever."

Despite all of Michael's foot-dragging, they eventually got married, and I saw them from time to time through the first eight years of their marriage. The last time they came in, they were about to move to New York City, where Michael had accepted an important position with a major publishing company. I expected him to be wracked by fears about his new job, the cross-country move, and everything else.

"So, Michael, how do you feel about moving?" I asked. "Are you nervous, anxious?"

"Not really," he said. "I look at it as an adventure. We've visited New York several times, and we love the energy and excitement there. Besides, if it doesn't work out, we can always move back."

Christine sat beside him, happy to let him do the talking. I noticed she didn't jump in and "pep him up" as she had before.

"How about your new job?" I asked him. "Sounds like a big step up for you."

"Yeah, it'll be a challenge, but I've come to enjoy challenges. It's kind of fun to put yourself in situations that force you to grow and develop. I'm pretty sure I'll be able to do a great job."

I was so surprised by Michael's newfound optimism that I had to ask about his marriage. "So tell me about you and Christine. Remember your reluctance to get married? What do you think now?"

"I think we're doing terrific," he replied without hesitation. "And looking back, I feel a little silly about how strongly I tried to talk us out of marrying. I suppose it's wise to be cautious, but it was obvious to everyone but me how *right* Christine and I were for each other." I noticed Christine grinning as Michael continued. "Oh, sure, we've had our struggles over the years like every couple, but nothing we couldn't handle. Our relationship keeps getting better and better."

What happened to this perpetual pessimist? It absolutely fascinated me that he had become a flaming optimist.

Why Did Michael Become an Optimist?

To understand why Michael became significantly more optimistic during his eight-year marriage to Christine, let's start with definitions. According to *Webster's Dictionary,* an *optimist* is a person who "has an inclination to put the most favorable construction upon actions and events or to anticipate the best possible outcome." On the other hand, a *pessimist* "has an inclination to emphasize adverse aspects, conditions, and possibilities or to expect the worst possible outcome." In both cases, they try to accurately predict a future outcome. The optimistic person heavily weighs factors that lend themselves to a positive prediction. Conversely, the pessimist emphasizes the negative data; thus, the prediction is negative.

There was no difference in Michael's and Christine's levels of intelligence. When making decisions, they usually made good ones. Both of them tried to make predictions on the basis of pertinent data. But Christine's optimism proved to be more influential over time because she was more often accurate in her predictions.

The reason has to do with the enormous potential of every person—the potential to change end results on the basis of highly motivated performance. If every person's performance is at least partly determined by his expectation of the eventual outcome, then an optimist's positive prediction of outcome is likely to produce a high performance level, and a pessimist's negative prediction is likely to produce a low level of performance.

We shouldn't assume that pessimists sabotage a process to prove the accuracy of their anticipated outcome. But we can assume that pessimists will not be motivated to try very hard. Their performance is likely to be far below their best. Since they don't expect a positive outcome, they have no reason to try for one. Partly because they have predicted a positive outcome, optimists will try hard to match their performance with their initial assessment of outcome.

Here's the bottom line: people tend to feel best about themselves when they operate at their highest levels. Thus, a positive prediction of outcome may produce their finest effort *and* result in their feeling most positively about themselves. It became obvious to me that Christine demonstrated these principles to Michael over time, and the attractiveness of her high performance and consistently high achievement made a convert out of him.

The Best Kind of Optimism Is Based on Reality

The secret of a great life is the ability to make consistently good judgments. In my book *Finding Contentment* (Thomas Nelson Publishers), I argue that "you can experience enduring contentment only when you have the courage to be deeply and profoundly your true self, the self you discover when you make careful and solid choices about your life all along the way."

Now, I am suggesting that being optimistic produces better health, better performance, better marriages, and better quality of life. But I want to make it clear that being an optimist is valuable only insofar as the optimism is grounded in good judgment. Optimism that lends itself to unrealistic expectations can do irreparable damage to individuals and marriages.

The key is to base your predictions about the future on the most positive data you have about the past and the present. You want your prediction to assume your finest effort because your eventual contentment depends on your being motivated to perform at that high level.

It needs to be clear, though, that every healthy optimist bases his outlook on the solid bedrock of a careful analysis of all relevant data. If his optimism becomes more wishful than reasonable, he is destined to be disappointed and disillusioned. There is nothing attractive about any person who consistently makes judgments about future outcomes that are excessively rosy and unattainable.

The most attractive people in the world are the thoughtful optimists who expect positive results based on high-level performance, performance that is predictable on the basis of fact and history.

What Makes Some People Optimists and Others Pessimists?

Considerable research evidence indicates that optimism and pessimism come from two primary sources. The first has to do with early childhood experiences. Children who endure hardship and tragedy—serious illness, divorce, violence, abuse—are highly prone to pessimistic thinking. On the other hand, children who grow up with encouraging, supportive parents, family cohesion, and personal achievements are likely to have an optimistic outlook.

The second source of optimism is what some writers have called the *parental explanatory style*. A study by Vanderbilt psychologist Judy Garber found that young adolescents frequently share the mother's outlook on life. They learn the mother's style of interpreting events, and they tend to predict similar results.

If children have been convinced that the setbacks and failures they encounter are the results of deficiencies in their makeup, they naturally become pessimistic about their chances of success in the future. On the other hand, clinical evidence demonstrates that when an adolescent believes he has the potential to succeed and that there is considerable room for improvement in his performance, his outlook becomes more and more optimistic.

Therefore, it is important to help every child and adolescent arrive at an accurate assessment of his potential. This directly relates to why it is so defeating to a child for a parent or person in authority to use negative, critical, blaming approaches in the management of his behavior. If the child or adolescent begins to diminish his own worth and potential, he will predict more and more negative outcomes for his efforts.

Expect Success—or Failure—and It's Likely to Happen

For more than three decades, research evidence has existed showing a close connection between expectation of an outcome and the actual outcome, especially for events in which the individual making the prediction is directly involved.

Robert Rosenthal of Harvard University conducted a fascinating study about expectations in the early 1960s. Experimenters were told that certain rats would learn to navigate a maze more rapidly because they were bred to be "maze bright," and other rats would perform more poorly because they were "maze dull." The "bright" rats did indeed perform at a higher level than the "dull" rats, even though they had all been randomly selected from a group of ordinary rats. The expectations of the experimenters significantly influenced the rats' learning pace.

In the human realm, it has frequently been shown that psychotherapy clients do better in therapy if their therapists initially believe that these clients will do better. My colleagues and I conducted research that demonstrated specific ways in which the expectations of therapists can be altered, and when they are, their clients progress faster and more successfully.

What you expect has a big influence on the final result of whatever your expectations are about. This is true even when your expectations involve someone else's behavior. It seems crucial in marriage, then, that you keep your expectations as positive as possible—that you become a profound optimist about everything that relates to you, your partner, and your life together.

Not surprisingly, research has also shown that pessimistic thinking often leads to failure. As early as 1965, Martin E. P. Seligman, one of America's most prominent psychologists, conducted research on what has been called *learned helplessness*.[1] This research demonstrated that when dogs become "convinced" that no effort on their part will change their helpless condition, they literally quit trying, and they show all the signs of discouragement and depression.

Seligman continued to improve these studies over time, and he became convinced that this condition of perceived helplessness in humans is a forerunner of depression. The depressive state results in generalized apathy, and under some conditions, the effort to reverse the expectancy is futile. Seligman connected this state of learned helplessness in humans to a pessimistic outlook.

Pessimism in Marriage

When one marriage partner is consistently pessimistic, the marriage is sure to ride like a bicycle with a flat tire. If pessimism is a sign that depression is close behind, then pessimism portends major marital trouble. No marriage can be happy if one person is chronically depressed. I often say, "No marriage can ever be healthier than the emotional health of the least healthy partner." Since depression is the major mental health problem in America, it is an enemy to every marriage. The best time to deal with it is before a person's pessimistic outlook becomes so habituated that it severely resists treatment of any kind.

Don't forget what pessimism is—a tendency "to emphasize adverse aspects . . . to expect the worst possible outcome." If you live with a person who is constantly pessimistic, your marriage will tend to become more and more constricted. One of you will put a damper on every idea. And one of you, the one who doesn't like these dampers, will grow progressively more restless and resentful.

I know a couple, Max and Sheila, who lived through

two decades during which one of them was an unwavering pessimist and the other was a confirmed optimist. Sheila was profoundly conservative, consistently cautious, and a naysayer about virtually everything. Her favorite phrases were, "We can't possibly do that!" and "It'll never work!" Max was a go-getter and a risk taker, whose schemes and dreams were often based more on fantasy than on reality.

How did these opposites get together in the first place? It was a textbook case of compensation—that is, they married each other to compensate for some of their individual deficiencies. Sheila married an optimist because she wanted to be set free from her chronically negative outlook on life. Max married a pessimist because he wanted help establishing boundaries around his excessive optimism. His irrational and illogical optimism often led to highly risky behavior. He believed far too strongly that his behavior would lead to positive outcomes. His frequent falling short of his predicted goals resulted in significant conflicts in their relationship.

Over time, Max's optimism scared Sheila so much that she became even more pessimistic and cautious. As you might expect, Max grew increasingly resentful that his wife held him back and rained on his parade. Eventually, he could take the straitjacket treatment no longer, and he began living life like a man released from a long prison sentence (which probably wasn't far from the truth). The problem was, his behavior became impulsive and erratic.

He pursued all kinds of extreme sports—skydiving, bungee jumping, parachuting off high cliffs. He invested their money in high-risk ventures. He got involved in out-landish business pursuits.

Their marriage on the verge of collapse, Max and Sheila realized that their wildly different perspectives were driving them farther and farther apart. With the help of a therapist and supportive friends, Max and Sheila tried to move from the outer edges to the middle—she trained herself to anticipate positive results in any situation, and he began thinking more practically and realistically. It wasn't easy! These patterns were so ingrained that it took many months, with numerous setbacks, before they achieved some equilibrium.

After a while, however, Max and Sheila came to view their previously adverse styles as an asset. When facing a challenge or opportunity, they would say to each other, "You can guess what I think about this, but what do *you* think?" As each grew to appreciate the other's viewpoint, their marriage flourished, and their effectiveness in life improved dramatically.

How Do You Become Optimistic?

If you or the love of your life desperately wants to be more optimistic, you're halfway there. The most striking fact about increasing optimism is that the decision to aim for it is under *your* control. If you decide to become more optimistic, you can be. You may need to make some adjustments in your thinking, but you can make these adjustments if you choose to.

After all, optimism—or pessimism—is *your* outlook on life. Its major function is to help you position yourself in relation to future events so that you have the maximum chance of success. Your definition of *success* will be determined by your values, and to some extent, your values flow from your life experience. Even your values can be rearranged if you decide to rearrange them.

Let me tell you where it all starts for me. Fundamental to the adoption of an optimistic outlook on your life is the need for a giant safety net. You need to know that you can make a few mistakes along the way and not be obliterated by them. If you adopt the right belief system, your mistakes will never render you unacceptable or worthless. You will still be a person of ultimate value. Without this safety net, your anxiety may run so high that you will protect yourself against every eventuality, safeguard yourself on every side, live every moment with ultimate caution, and play for a 0–0 tie in the game of life.

Pessimism reflects the conviction and determination to never fail. Indeed, I know many people who have never failed. They go through life without a single failure! But neither do they ever succeed. Their pessimism protects them perfectly from failure, but their lack of optimism bars them from abundant life.

What is this safety net I'm referring to? For me, it is a spiritual matter. It has to do with my sense of being in a right relationship with God. I think of God as the man Jesus, the Jewish Carpenter. Jesus' message is full of all the qualities I admire in God and humans: love, forgiveness, encouragement, and hope. When I am spiritually alive in relation to Jesus, I am deeply aware of my total personal security—now and eternally. I know myself to be personally loved, forgiven, encouraged, and allowed to be hopeful. I have a safety net for living my life.

Healthy optimism, then, leads me to put the most favorable construction on future actions and events. It causes me to anticipate the best possible outcome. I want to make predictions that will require my finest effort. I want to have to give every last ounce of energy. If my predictions are accurate, my life will be all that it can be. I will achieve my goals, and equally important, I will experience the thrill of giving a maximum effort. And if I miss, I have a safety net!

How Do Safety Nets Relate to Marriage?

Because Marylyn and I are aware that we have the same safety net, we are prepared to assess the likely outcome of any marital process with maximum optimism and courage. For instance, when we determine goals for the future, the amount of money we will give away to those less fortunate, or the friends we will cultivate, we will make choices together that are permeated with optimism.

I remember one of our most pivotal moments. Years ago, we were trying to decide whether we should buy a particular house. We didn't know whether we could afford it. In my compulsive way, I made every kind of chart. I formed long pro and con lists. I consulted every wise person we knew. We studied all the ramifications of buying this house from every perspective. After all this fact-finding and soul-searching, I was leaning toward a negative decision because the transaction would have pushed us to the edge of our financial comfort zone.

But then Marylyn made a powerful and influential observation: "We have made more money each year until now, and we are likely to continue doing so. Because we can afford the house even if our income stays the same, and because we are likely to make more in the future, I think we ought to go ahead and buy it."

We did, and in retrospect, she was absolutely right. We ended up thoroughly enjoying the house, and it proved to be a good investment. Again and again, we have profited from Marylyn's optimism. I'm not saying the optimist will always be right. But I've come to believe that when facing a problem or decision, you should tilt your thinking in the direction of the optimist's point of view.

The Purpose of Life and the Role of Optimism

When two married people are freed from their compulsive need not to fail, and when they make predictions about the future that require their best efforts, they are poised to experience the finest living available to human beings.

Remember that optimism must always be based on a careful assessment of what your judgment will require of you. It must never be governed by mere fantasy or wishful thinking. It should always be the result of prudent and careful analysis.

And when it is, your marriage will be supercharged with hopefulness and confidence. If you accurately position yourselves on the optimism-pessimism continuum, your very best effort will be required to reach your goal. Nothing in life should be allowed to rob you of your free and positive predictions about a marital life that requires your best and fulfills you at your deepest levels.

5

Invigorate Your Marriage with Inspirational Moments

One summer afternoon several years ago, Marylyn and I watched the movie *Father of the Bride,* which was filmed near our home in Pasadena, California. Many of you already know the story. A dad and mom go through the excruciating experience of watching their "little girl" fall in love with a systems analyst and prepare for marriage. The film is about the passing of time, the aging of children and their parents, and the enormous emotional challenge for parents as they adapt to their child becoming an adult, asserting independence, and leaving the nest.

It was painfully easy for me to identify with the father in this film. With three daughters of our own, daughters we have cherished from the moment of their births, I was a sitting duck for the emotional tug of this story.

Steve Martin played the dad in the movie, and as soon as he learned that his daughter was in love with "this other man," his symptoms began. Threatened with the loss of his daughter, he couldn't hold his conscious focus on her as a grown-up. When he looked at her across the dinner table or on the basketball court, he kept seeing her as she was as a seven- or eight-year-old. He suffered, of course, from his unconscious need to keep her small— safely and forever "under the shadow of his wing." He didn't like being reminded that she had become an adult. He was forced to reckon with the anxiety-laden, age-old problem of the inexorable passage of time.

I watched intently as Martin writhed through all his anguish, and I experienced one wave of powerful emotion after another. It suddenly occurred to me that it was only a short time ago—just a few weeks ago, wasn't it?—that our girls were young and impressionable and blissfully playing with Barbies. It was perhaps a couple of days ago that they were rah-rahing as high school cheerleaders, and I'm sure it was just yesterday that we drove each of them off to college.

In reality, they aren't "girls" anymore. They are moms with little ones of their own. "How did these years fly by so fast?" I asked.

The movie demanded that I recognize all over again the obvious truth: all that we have together with our loved ones cannot be detached from rapidly passing time. There is no *necessary* grief attached to this powerful principle, but to make peace with passing time, we must stay constantly alert, uncommonly focused, and as utterly present as possible at each moment. The only successful antidote for losing time is living and experiencing fully that time now—while it is the present.

In *that* moment, the inspiration I felt gave me a clearer perspective about the vital importance of *all* my moments, and I was struck by newfound passion to live these moments with maximum personal investment.

As I struggled to process all these weighty matters during the movie, I glanced over at Marylyn in her big chair, and I could see through my tears that she was crying too.

"What are you crying about?" I asked.

She told me about her own sense of grief that our children are all grown up, and she shared her motivation to make the most of all our moments. Then she startled me with an insight of a totally different variety. "I'm crying because you're crying," she said.

Her sense of partnership with me is so well established that we now feel each other's feelings. Think of it! For a lot of reasons, including the fact that we are inspired by the same events many times, my wife and I are developing one heart for the two of us. Our blending is creating a bond a hundred times stronger than the strongest epoxy.

Whenever the two of us have an inspirational experience together, our marriage is destined to become richer, and the two of us are certain to be more woven together at our deepest levels.

Why Inspirational Experiences Create
So Much Marital Bonding

One of the central meanings of the word *inspire* is "to breathe into or upon." The air you breathe is obviously crucial to the continuance of your life, so to be inspired is a matter of life-sustaining importance. But two additional points provide insights for us.

First, the air you breathe is remarkably intimate to you. It literally becomes a part of you. It circulates throughout your bloodstream. Thus, the nature of this air—where it has been and what it has been used for—is critical to you. The source of your "inspiration" will partially, even largely, determine the quality of your experience.

Second, if what inspires you becomes woven into the fabric of your being, it is vital to choose the sources of these inspirational events carefully. If you can be inspired by a thousand different people, ideas, events, or even dreams, the ones you choose to transfuse into your emotional heart and brain will have a gigantic influence on the shape of your life.

Applying these characteristics of inspiration to marriage, we realize that (1) every married couple needs to select inspirational sources that will contribute to the long-term health of life together; and (2) these sources have the most potent effect on marriage when they are experienced in the same way for both married partners.

Four of My Most Inspirational Events

We encounter inspiring events every day. Some are relatively small—watching a mother sensitively care for her handicapped child, hearing a beautiful song in church, receiving an encouraging note from a friend. Others are monumental and unforgettable, such as the four I want to share with you. The first involves Martin Luther King Jr., who was by far the most inspirational speaker I ever heard. Marylyn and I first heard Dr. King on television in Chicago in 1962 on the *Chicago Sunday Evening Club*. We were both awestruck by his eloquence and power. We talked about little else for days afterward. The fact that he was so deeply committed to nonviolence during a highly violent period had a life-changing effect on our own approach to social change.

One of the most inspirational experiences of my life was watching Dr. King deliver his now-famous "I Have a Dream" speech before the Lincoln Memorial in August 1963. He pleaded for justice and freedom for his people—and all people—with a passion few of us had ever witnessed. I have watched a film of that speech again and again, and to this day I get goose bumps every time I relive it.

The speech is spectacularly stirring because of its magnificent craftsmanship. It strikes me as a brilliant composition—poetic, persuasive, powerful, and sweepingly for and about *all* Americans. It sets forth the truth—not just the truth as Dr. King saw it, but the truth as a vast majority of Americans saw it.

The speech is also inspirational because of its unassailable idealism. Focusing on young children as it did, King's speech advanced ideals that took on unparalleled purity. His arguments had the power of "right" behind them and omitted even a hint of anything violent, militaristic, or threatening.

When couples sit together and share inspiring moments like this one was for Marylyn and me, their marriage will be invigorated and impassioned. Inspiring events have that effect on partners. Imagine, for instance, that million-person crowd during the last third of Dr. King's speech, cheering as one voice, yet listening intently. King boldly and poetically spun their hopes and dreams as he set forth his beliefs and convictions:

> With this faith we will be able to hew out of the mountain of despair a stone of hope. With this faith we will be able to transform the jangling discords of our nation into a beautiful symphony of brotherhood. With this faith we will be able to work together, to pray together,

to struggle together, to go to jail together, to stand up for freedom together, knowing that we will be free one day. This will be the day when all of God's children will be able to sing with new meaning: "My country, 'tis of thee, sweet land of liberty, of thee I sing. Land where my fathers died, land of the pilgrim's pride, from every mountainside, let freedom ring!" And if America is to be a great nation, this must become true.

Now that's what I call inspirational! When you "breathe in" these ideals as a couple, your individual and collective lives are bound to become richer and fuller, deeper and more fulfilling.

Obviously, inspirational events for an individual or couple needn't be so grand and national in scope. They may take place on a comparatively tiny stage with the slightest of fanfare.

Marylyn and I had been married two years when we decided to move from California to Chicago so I could pursue graduate training in psychology. We were poorer than church mice, with our wedding gifts our only worldly possessions. Two days before we made our trip, my mother recognized that we were suitcase deprived. She came to us and said, "I have decided to use my stamps for a new bag for each of you."

Let me tell you why that offer represented one of the

most inspirational events of my life. My depression-bred mother had saved S & H Green Stamps for many years. I never gave it much thought, but I knew that she had dozens of green stamp books and that she spent hours pasting the stamps into these books.

"Mom, no!" I immediately responded. "You should buy yourself something nice with all that saving and hard work you've done."

Despite my protests, she gathered those books of stamps the next day and, with my dad's help, set off for the S & H Redemption Store. She traded in those stamps for two full-size Samsonite cases, a beautiful white one for her daughter-in-law and a gorgeous charcoal-colored one for her departing son.

Why did that event inspire Marylyn and me so much? Because my mother's giving was sacrificial and pure, a clear, heartfelt expression of her love for us—a love that neither of us ever doubted during the years of her life.

The third event I find unusually inspirational happened to a couple named James and Arlene Loder. I have met Jim Loder on only a few occasions, but I've never met Arlene. Nevertheless, a powerful story from their lives has had a deep impact on Marylyn and me.

Headed on a road trip from Princeton, New Jersey, to Quebec, Canada, the Loders and their two daughters stopped to help an older woman whose car was disabled by a flat tire. As Jim set about replacing the woman's tire, a man in another car traveling in the same direction went to sleep at the wheel, veered off the road, and slammed into the car that Jim was trying to fix. Trapped with the front of the woman's car on his chest, Jim was severely injured, and he called desperately for help. His wife was the only person within earshot who could offer assistance.

Arlene is a slight woman, barely over five feet tall, but her husband's life depended on her freeing him from beneath the car. With her hands under the bumper, she lifted with all her strength as she prayed, "In the name of Jesus Christ, in the name of Jesus Christ . . ." Recounting this event later, she said that when her strength began to give way, she partially lost consciousness for a few seconds. When she was able to refocus her attention, she was surprised to see that the car had been lifted.

Why do we find this event so inspiring? First, Jim Loder lived because Arlene gave every last ounce of energy she had to give—even more energy than her body could afford. But also because in this experience, one small woman's almost superhuman strength, needed desperately by the man she loved most, became surprisingly available.

And finally, Marylyn and I were moved because Dr. James Loder wrote a book called *The Transforming Moment* about the monumental impact this experience had on his life. This professor at Princeton Theological

Seminary has helped shape thousands of lives through the years, and this near-tragic event played a critical role in the extension of his influence and the formulation of his entire life perspective.

The last event I want to mention is the horrible South Dakota plane crash that claimed the life of golf pro Payne Stewart, whose funeral provided inspiration for millions of married couples worldwide. The source of this inspiration? The marital and family story of Payne and Tracey Stewart.

The memorial service was held in Orlando, Florida, with an estimated three thousand persons in attendance, including more than eighty professional golfers. Tracey Stewart, with her brother at her side for strength, shared her recollections of Payne. The account of the funeral was told magnificently by J. A. Adande of the *Los Angeles Times:*

> She spoke of what was gained by his presence, not what was lost by his death. "I feel that I have been blessed by God," she said. "I thank Him for allowing me to share the last 18 years of my life with Payne."
>
> Tracey Stewart told a love story, their love story, simple and pure. Their eyes first met from across the room at a cocktail party during an event in Australia.
>
> "I didn't even know what his name was," Tracey said. All she knew was that he was the most beautiful man she had ever seen. "From the night of the first date,

I can honestly tell you, that this was the man I wanted to share my life with."

After thanking some close friends and "all the people everywhere for their heartfelt prayers and sympathy," she turned her attention to her husband.

"Finally, I thank God for Payne," she said. "We shared laughter, tears, victories, and defeats. You will always be my soulmate and my best friend. You are the light of my life and my tower of strength. You'll live in my heart forever . . . I realize that even after 18 years of marriage, Payne was still the most beautiful man I'd ever seen. Not because of the way he looked on the outside anymore, but because of what was on the inside. We love you . . . let the party in heaven begin."[1]

I'm not sure there are any marriage partners alive who, after hearing all that, would not be inspired to live out their partnership with greater attention to the spouse's feelings and needs.

Paul Azinger, the professional golfer and Payne Stewart's close friend, also spoke at the funeral. Before he shared his thoughts with the congregation, "he slipped on one of Stewart's trademark caps and rolled up the pants of his suit and tucked them into knee-high argyle socks to mimic Stewart's famous knickers. Azinger's attire was so appropriately inappropriate that the mourners couldn't help but respond with an act that also is normally out of place at such a function: They applauded."

After Azinger told about Stewart's "crazier" side, he talked about the progress Stewart made as a person:

> For many years it seemed like Payne Stewart was first in Payne Stewart's life. But long ago that began to change. We all saw his pride and occasional cynicism and sarcasm begin to soften. Payne became gracious in victory and gracious in defeat. Only God can do that, because only God can change hearts . . . It should not be viewed as a coincidence that the resurgence in Stewart's career came after he de-emphasized golf and began focusing on his faith and his family.

What else can I say about the powerful effect of inspirational life events on the growth of a marital relationship? Only this: whenever you and the love of your life sit together and hear Ray Charles sing "America" and you hold each other as tightly as you know how, whenever you hear a great athlete take the time to salute parents or grandparents for their life-changing influence and you sense again the deep debt we owe those who gave sacrificially of themselves in order for us to have life and opportunity, whenever the two of you hear the first cry of a baby or watch two older persons support each other in a time of need, whenever inspiration graces your life together, recognize this as one of God's powerful ways of bonding you together so strongly that you can survive every twist of fate for as long as you live.

What Inspirational Events Have in Common

When we look at all these inspirational events, what do they have in common? First, the matter of unselfishness comes to mind. Could it be that the finest human attribute is unselfishness? Being selfish isn't a horrible problem, but there is something wonderful about not needing to be. Maybe truly unselfish people are inspiring to us because they have learned the secret of satisfying their deepest personal needs and are therefore able to focus on the needs of others.

Another aspect common to inspirational events has to do with getting it right. Martin Luther King was all about trying to get it right. He recognized that racial inequality was dead wrong, and he needed to help change the country's attitude. He knew, of course, that bending a social system back into the "right" position was going to produce pain before it produced the eventual consequences of "rightness."

Further, King tried to set things right the right way. In other words, he didn't right one wrong by creating another wrong. He refused to stir up violence. He called the attention of millions of Americans to serious societal wrongs, and he marshaled public opinion against these wrongs, but he categorically refused to fight fire with fire. He inspired us to recognize that we are capable of a higher wisdom and a far more unselfish courage.

Inspiration, then, usually relates to the spotlighting of great values. When we see these values lifted up, we are encouraged to lift them up in our own marriages. And in this process, our life together takes on a new vibrancy and beauty.

One more observation on the process of inspiring each other to a better bonded marital relationship: events that build up our marriages often come from other marriages we admire. We are moved as we witness a wife tenderly caring for her seriously ill husband. We draw courage from couples who summon all their strength to prevail over a family tragedy. Our spirits are lifted when we hear of a husband who makes great sacrifices so his wife can achieve a long-sought goal. If these other marriages give evidence of growth on the basis of qualities available to all of us, they provide tremendous inspiration for us.

Paul Azinger told us that the Stewarts had gotten it together as a couple and a family only when Payne had gotten his own priorities in order. When Azinger said, "It should not be viewed as a coincidence that the resurgence in Stewart's career came after he de-emphasized golf and began focusing on his faith and his family," he emboldened many spouses to follow that example.

I couldn't help being doubly impressed with the *Los Angeles Times* article's follow-up paragraph, synchronized as it is with the entire message of this book: "Golf is funny that way. If you try to crush the ball, you'll knock it into the woods. But a nice, easy swing will send the ball sailing down the middle of the fairway. Stewart had learned to relax and let everything come to him."

The fact that the Stewarts had learned to do this is a major part of the inspirational power of this story. The fact that their marital relationship had become so extraordinary generates even greater passion in us to follow their lead.

The Four Most Powerful Values
Involved with Inspiration

As I have studied the subject of inspiration, I have noticed that four values continually appear—values that can give couples strength to draw from.

1. Persistence

If you study the lives of inspirational people, you will consistently encounter an emphasis on never giving up. Great human beings often become great because they refuse to throw in the towel. My favorite "persister" is Winston Churchill. It took him three years to get through the eighth grade because he had trouble learning English grammar. At one point in his educational career, he was dead last in his class, and his father literally gave up on him. When we consider how influential he was in determining the outcome of World War II, we are extremely fortunate that Churchill persevered.

Robert Service was a poet I read as a kid. He wrote plain old rhyming poetry. One stanza from Service's poem "The Quitter" has never left me:

> It's the plugging away that will win you the day,
> So don't be a piker, old pard!
> Just draw on your grit; it's so easy to quit;
> It's the keeping-your-chin-up that's hard.[2]

I can assure you that in my thirty-five years of marriage counseling, I've seen some incredible examples of persistence. I've watched marriages that I thought were goners rise from near death to become fully alive and energized. On the other hand, I have witnessed far too many spouses give up on their marriage at too early a point. A little more tenacity could have turned things around.

2. *Courage*

Courage is often borne of one's deep commitment to something or someone. For instance, when it comes to our three daughters, I would gladly risk my life for a chance of

saving theirs. The same is true of my wife. If I saw a car speed-
ing toward her, I would lunge to push her out of harm's way,
even if that meant getting run over myself.

When it comes to marriage, I have watched courage
play a significant role for many spouses. Many of the
couples I've worked with over the years have courageously
defended their marriage when some person or force
sought to destroy it. Sometimes a parent tries to drive a
wedge between a husband and a wife. Sometimes a troubled teenager can lead parents to blame each other and
become opponents instead of allies. Sometimes a debilitat-
ing illness threatens the stability of a marriage. Couples in
these situations need a reservoir of courage so they can
stand firm against anything that would undermine their
relationship.

3. Generosity

I have watched marriages become inspired because
of the generosity of one of the partners or because the
spouses witnessed someone else's sacrificial generosity.

I am often moved by the generosity of mothers I know
who give their children or husbands virtually everything
they have to give, often at high cost to themselves. Their
generosity seems to be derived from their deep love for their
family. What an inspiration this is for me to give liberally to
those I love.

4. *Idealism*

There is something deep within most human beings that makes us want to reach for our ideals. We yearn to be the best we can be, even when no one else knows how hard we try at any given time. And we like to see others reach for high ideals in their lives too. We want to believe that as a human race, all people are capable of being noble, selfless, fair, and truthful.

Sometimes the pursuit of idealism is played out in big, public venues—the Olympic arena, the battlefield, the courthouse. But the best places I have found to look for idealism are on the little stages of life, the locations where no one knows he is being observed and certainly not studied. For instance, elevators are places to watch for selflessness. How eager is someone to help another passenger who has his hands full? How patiently does one respond when a slow, elderly couple shuffle in and take a few moments to remember which floor they're going to? How encouraging does an individual treat the harried mother with three rambunctious kids?

When I'm out with Marylyn, I like to note examples of idealistic behavior: the kindness of others, their special efforts to help out, their willingness to give unselfishly. And I try to speak to these people. I thank them and tip them well; I write letters to their superiors and go out of my way to express my appreciation for them.

When Marylyn and I watch a person trying to do the right thing, trying to be his best, we glance at each other with knowing expressions. We communicate, "We should do the same! With each other, with our family, with strangers, we should always strive to be the best we can be." When we focus our consciousness on the idealism of others, we are encouraged to pursue idealism in our marriage.

A Final Word About the Role of Inspiration in Strengthening Marriage

There are many ways to make a marriage stronger, some far more effective than others. One proven approach to the bonding and blending of marital partners is for the two of them to collectively experience life events that are mutually uplifting to their spirits. This seldom happens when there develops between them an unhealthy focus on problems, issues, deficits, and challenges.

Every couple on earth deserves to have a supporting cast of caring persons who demonstrate the high ideals about which we have been talking. The goal is to imbue this couple with ample evidence that noble values can characterize the relationship, that unselfishness, sensitivity, and kindness can consistently prevail in their life together.

The apostle Paul in the New Testament has a word for couples at the end of his letter to the church at Philippi:

Fix your thoughts on what is true and good and right.
Think about things that are pure and lovely, and dwell
on the fine, good things in others. Think about all you
can praise God for and be glad about. Keep putting into
practice all you learned from me and saw me doing, and
the God of peace will be with you. (Phil. 4:8–9 TLB)

There is no question about it: when married couples
watch for inspirational people and events, they are
strengthened. But when they obsess over the problems,
they are torn apart.

I choose to keep thinking about the courage of Martin
Luther King Jr., the simple love and sensitivity of my
mother, the unlikely strength of a tiny person like Arlene
Loder when her husband's life was at stake, and the beautiful marital relationship of Payne and Tracey Stewart.

My clinical experience fills me with this sure confidence: spouses who regularly experience inspiring events
together will have an inspirational marriage that grows
more and more in beauty and love.

6

Accentuate Your Marriage with Abundant Physical Affection

Kevin and Margie live in a small town in Ohio, and they attended one of my marriage seminars in Dayton. After my talk on marital sex, Margie stood in line to have me sign one of my books. Because I speak openly and frankly about sexuality, people don't mind being open with me in return. In a matter of ninety seconds, Margie told me a fascinating story about the importance of "the physical" in their marriage.

"Kevin and I love to be physical with each other," Margie said, "and we take every opportunity to be in touch with each other."

I thought for sure I was going to hear another dramatic account of a highly charged, highly sexed American couple who have had sex every day since they were married twenty years ago. I get stories like that once in a while, but that wasn't at all the case with Margie and Kevin.

"We cuddle frequently during the night, and we hug each other when we wake up in the morning," she said.

"We purposely run into each other when we're taking our showers and dressing, and we stand close when we're grabbing a quick bite and a cup of coffee. We hug before we leave for work, and we hold each other a little when we get home. We give each other shoulder rubs while we're cooking our dinner, and we sit together in one big chair while we watch our favorite TV shows."

Then she summed it all up: "Kevin and I have found that a lot of touching helps bind us together emotionally, so we make the most of it."

I finished signing her book, and then I asked a question that suddenly occurred to me: "Not to be nosy, but is all this touching in place of sex, or do you have sex too?"

Margie looked a little surprised at my candor. But she smiled and said, "Oh, we have good sex, but sex is just a part of all the touching we do."

I vividly recall this woman's story because it came just a week after I heard a far different tale. A fiftyish couple who had been married twenty-three years came to my office for counseling, and when they arrived, I couldn't help observing the three feet of space between them as they sat rigidly on my couch (psychologists notice these things!).

Before I could ask what brought them to my office, the woman announced in a voice that sounded like scraping sandpaper, "Our marriage has never been what you'd call affectionate. But now Roger hardly ever touches me.

Hardly ever! It's as if I have some skin disease he thinks he's going to catch from me." Then she leaned forward and said in a conspiratorial tone, "We do have, you know, intercourse, probably, oh, once or twice a month, but that's clearly for Roger's benefit—if you get my drift. The man is a cold fish, Dr. Warren. A cold fish!"

Poor Roger sank a little lower into the couch cushions and looked as if he was going to be ill. I asked him for his take on the situation. He sighed heavily and said, "It's true—the part about us not being very affectionate. I'm just not a touchy-feely man. I try, I really do, but it's just not in my nature. But she"—he stabbed his finger in the air in his wife's direction—"she doesn't make it easy. Always criticizing my attempts at affection and calling me derisive names—'ice cube,' 'fence post,' 'cold fish.'"

They spent the next fifteen minutes telling me how their marriage had grown progressively listless and lifeless, how their marital satisfaction had devolved along with the quantity and quality of their physical affection.

Ah, yes, what a difference touching—or its lack—makes in marriages. No doubt Roger and his wife had problems that more hugging and kissing wouldn't resolve, but a little more tenderness might have created an environment in which they could address their issues. What I told this couple—and what I certainly didn't need to tell Margie and Kevin—was that touching turns up the temperature in a marriage. It creates warmth and closeness. Of all the skills that can enhance a relationship, it is one of the easiest to learn.

How about you and your lover? Would you consider yourselves exceedingly, moderately, or infrequently affectionate with each other? Do you regularly hug, hold hands, smooch, walk arm in arm? Are you all over each other or rarely close to each other? For every married couple, touching is a ready-made reservoir of relational energy and intimacy. The key is learning to maximize this resource.

The Rewards of Abundant Physical Affection

Two married people who enjoy touching each other find dozens of ways to communicate their love every day. Physical touching is a magnificent channel for deep and meaningful communication. For some couples, more feelings and messages are transmitted physically than verbally. And if you become adept at deciphering "physical code," you can carry on long conversations without saying a word.

There is not a thing in the world wrong with sexual communication, but it is much more complex, and it requires elaborate preparations to make sure both people are ready for it. Good sex can merge two lovers at the deep-down soul level, and it can take you right into the presence of God. But by the very nature of its complexity, good sex for most couples is not going to happen every day—and maybe not every week or month.

Good touching is much more available and accessible. You may not be able to send the powerful, soul-reverberating messages that you can with sex, but you can send a lot more of them at a fraction of the emotional-stress cost. And it may well be that the quantity of touching more than makes up for the intensity of intercourse.

Abundant physical affection brings a lighter touch to marriage in two ways. First, it takes the burden off your sex life. That is, many couples place enormous pressure on themselves to have ecstatic sex every time they climb between the sheets. When their sex life becomes a little blasé or unexciting, they wonder what's wrong with them. But when you view sex as a part of your overall physical relationship, you place less weight on this one aspect.

Second, lots of touching increases the chances for better sex. Touching fosters closeness, and without closeness sex is sure to be unsatisfying. I'm always amazed when couples can't figure out why their sex life is not more gratifying—even though they rarely touch each other except during intercourse. Caressing, hugging, cuddling, and holding hands are great warm-ups for sex. This isn't to say that all touching should lead to sex, but affection enhances the mood for lovemaking.

Obviously, sex is an important component of any married couple's love relationship. But there is so much more to physical affection than intercourse, and there are so many rewards to be gained by making touch of every kind a frequent and abundant part of your lives. I encourage couples to master their physical relationship. I assure them that this is a lot bigger and a lot easier area to master than their sexual relationship. And the potential for fun and relational growth is enormous.

Why Touch Sends Such a Powerful Message

When someone touches you in a warm and affectionate way, you assume that he likes you, that he wants to be in touch with you. I suppose it is human nature not to enjoy touching people you don't like; you don't want to be close to people you find offensive or off-putting. But when you really like someone, you put an arm around him, you hold on to her hand longer when you shake it, or you reach out and gently grab his shoulder. It is an automatic way of saying, "I like you, I'm glad to be with you, I enjoy being in your presence, and I feel close to you."

Some people can deepen a relationship through the words they say and the conversations in which they engage. But words are more difficult for other people, and touching is more natural and meaningful to them. And the right kind of touching is incredibly powerful in conveying deep feelings and meanings. There is something about skin on skin that is intimate and able to communicate messages at an almost unconscious level.

Consider the power of a common handshake. It is a rare case indeed that you meet a stranger or encounter an old friend without reaching out to shake the person's hand. It's almost as if you are telling the individual that you are delighted to see her, that you have good intentions toward her, and she can touch your skin to gauge your sincerity level.

Dozens of important messages are transmitted when your skin touches someone else's skin. The body's temperature carries one or more of these messages, and the dryness or dampness of the skin carries others. Moreover, the appropriateness of the grip—too firm, too limp, or just right—will indicate the level of interpersonal security and peacefulness.

When it comes to marital touching, a spouse can communicate feelings in countless ways. Think about the act of kissing. When the lips of one person touch the lips of another, an enormous number of nerve endings are electrified. All kinds of things about each person are being shared with the other. And should the tongues become involved, even more nerve endings are ready to register the content of the message.

Marylyn always comments on how much she likes it when I rub her shoulders. She considers it a sacrificial offering on my part. The fact is, I love rubbing her shoulders. When she lets me know how much she enjoys it, I am motivated to rub her shoulders longer and more skillfully. It is a way that I can touch her so that she understands better the depth of my love for her.

Touching Fosters Talking

Two "lightbulb" experiences helped me realize the power of touch, both of which came when Marylyn and I lived in Chicago years ago. The first occurred when our three daughters were young. Marylyn and I noted that bedtime was the most important teaching time of the day, so we began to give special emphasis to it. We went to the bedside of each daughter every night, which quickly became a meaningful ritual.

The bedtimes always included a cup of water or milk, and we sang all kinds of songs, especially the ones they had learned at Sunday school. And we prayed with them—rote prayers in the beginning that became more and more spontaneous and personal as the girls grew.

But the part of the process that most grabbed my attention was our talks with them. I'd like to say that my psychological training led me to this profound communication technique, but I happened upon it by chance. As I sat on my daughters' beds and spoke quietly with them, I would ask, "Do you want me to rub your back and shoulders?" Without saying a word, they would turn over on their stomachs as a clear signal of their wishes. At first, we gave them relatively short massages, the kind Marylyn and I often gave to each other, but then we began to see the light. The more we rubbed their backs, the more relaxed they became; the more relaxed they became, the more freely they communicated with us. As long as we kept rubbing their necks and backs, they kept letting us in on their thoughts, feelings, and dreams. Back rubs came to be the most important part of going to bed.

Since our relationship with each of these "girls" (now grown women) continues to be close and meaningful to this day, I attribute a lot of credit to those bedtime talks we used to have with them.

Naturally, this principle holds as true for marriage as it does for child rearing. Think back on some of the good talks you and your partner have had recently. Chances are, some touching was involved. Perhaps you were sitting close on the couch, snuggling by the fire, holding hands as you walked through the park, or exchanging back rubs before bedtime. If you can't recall any good talks, use this principle as an experiment: the next time you and your lover are chatting, scoot close, hold hands, rub his or her shoulders—and see if your conversation isn't a little more open, free-flowing, and substantial.

Soul-Level Communication Happens Most Often Through Physical Touch

The second powerful lesson I learned about touch came when Marylyn and I attended a church in which there were twenty or thirty men and women who could not speak or hear. All services were translated for them through sign language. We struggled at first to make our inner meanings clear to them and to understand theirs. But over time, Marylyn and I came to know many of these people well. And even though verbal symbols were absent, we learned to interpret, and then to send, our thoughts and feelings to each other in other ways. Touching was the best of these ways.

These individuals—with disabled mouths and ears—were masterful at telling us how much they cared for us. It was as though their souls were directly connected to their hands and their bodies. When their skin touched our skin, they somehow verbalized a message that was crystal clear in both its intensity and its specificity. It was as though they had learned to share on the soul level with each other, and then with us, in a way that few hearing and speaking persons had learned.

Out of that six-year experience came an entirely new appreciation for Marylyn and me about the powerful role of touching in our marriage. We came to believe that many of our deepest thoughts and feelings about each other cannot be communicated through simple words and sounds. They need a more powerful language. They need the language of touch.

That is why sexuality has such a significant place in conveying love. Without any words, the lovemaking involved in sexuality can tell an inner story so powerfully that it binds one soul to another. I am convinced that the full sharing of marital love requires mastering the art of physical touch.

When you really love another person, it isn't easy to tell him in a way that matches the depth of your feeling. Words are vital, but they are almost never sufficient. These soul-centered inner feelings require the warmth of cheeks touching cheeks, lips touching lips, bodies holding bodies, hands holding hands—touching of every kind as frequently as possible. This is the only way to convince each other of undying love and eternal commitment.

Romance, Physical Expression, and Sexuality

I've alluded to the fact that touching, romance, and satisfying sex are interconnected. Lots of warm, affectionate touching promotes romance, and romance promotes great sex. Touching and other acts of romance disclose to your partner your deepest feelings of love, care, and commitment. When the souls of two lovers are full of unselfish and committed feelings, and when they have managed to convey these positive sentiments to each other, they are ready for the most sublime form of human touching and marital bonding.

Marital sexuality between two persons whose lives are intertwined is the most intimate form of love communication. It allows both persons to share from the deepest parts of their souls. And when you get this ultimate form of touching right in your relationship, it is a strong indication that you have successfully gone through all the preliminary steps involved in the physical communication of your love.

The truth that good sex depends on a soul connection between two partners cannot be overemphasized. To make marital sex work well, you need harmony of the soul and the body.

I saw a woman in therapy named Monica, who complained that she and her husband were totally out of sync in their sexual life.

"Brad complains that I'm shut down sexually," Monica said in a low voice, "and I guess he's right. I haven't had very much interest in sex since early in our marriage. But from my point of view, Brad sends me mixed messages."

There was a long silence, and I waited for Monica to order her thoughts. After a few moments, she said, "I'm just not convinced that he really loves me, that he is connected with me at the deepest of levels, and until I'm confident of that, I don't feel safe with him sexually."

"Well," I asked, "have you and Brad ever had a good sexual relationship, one in which both of you felt in sync with each other and both of you got your deepest needs satisfied?"

"We did in the beginning," Monica said. "Brad used to spend so much time with me and tell me what was going on inside him. He would hold me for hours, spin out his dreams for our future together, share his total commitment and loyalty to me. I felt so wonderful with him."

"What happened to interrupt all this wonderful sharing and togetherness?" I asked her.

She thought for a while and then said, "We were both working, and as we became more successful in our jobs, we invested less time and energy in each other. We sort of drifted apart. Over time, I came to know Brad less and less well."

"And so that's when your sex life began to deteriorate?"

"I wouldn't use the word *deteriorate*," Monica said as she looked up at me. "It was worse than that—it was more like our sex life ended."

I have heard similar stories a hundred times in my practice. It has to do with a woman's need to feel safe in relation to a man, to experience him as deeply in love with and connected to her, to know in her bones and her muscles that he is committed to her for a lifetime. When she begins to lose touch with his inner world, her sense of safety rapidly evaporates. Sexual involvement makes her feel vulnerable, and she doesn't want to feel that vulnerable with someone she senses is the least bit indifferent or noncommittal toward her. Sexuality magnifies a woman's strongest feelings—vulnerability or security, distance or closeness.

Monica was awash in her experience of vulnerability. I told her, "I can sense your hurt and frustration over your lack of sexual intimacy, but I believe your trouble in this area is a symptom of a larger problem. Your relationship with Brad lacks closeness and warmth, so how can you expect to experience bliss in your marriage bed? The good news is, I strongly suspect that when you and Brad get reconnected—when your love and romance are rekindled—your sexual problems will for the most part take care of themselves."

A Sense of Commitment Is Key to a Woman's Sexual Satisfaction

Since a woman bears children, and since having children becomes such a complex and consuming part of her life, she is consciously or unconsciously motivated to make sure that her sexual involvement is founded on durable love. If it is not, her sense of risk will overwhelm her; she will at some level of her being recognize the enormous responsibility of rearing children all by herself.

If a woman does not believe that a man's most basic thoughts and feelings indicate his enduring partnership with her over time, she automatically becomes sexually defensive and protective. I realize that many women misread men's true feelings and intentions or are taken in by false promises. But the fact remains—a woman instinctively wants to give her body only to a man she trusts will be with her over the long haul.

To deal effectively with her vulnerability, a woman may beg for more communication from her man. She wants her husband to let her know what is happening on the inside, especially as those thoughts and feelings relate to their mutual partnership, to their love relationship. A woman knows at a fundamental level that the sexual relationship should be only as strong as the love commitment.

Sometimes a man has a deep and loving commitment to his wife, but he shows it in a totally inadequate way. When you come right down to it, a woman's full involvement in the sexual relationship often depends on the degree to which the man has persuaded her of his love and long-term commitment.

It may be more true for a woman than for a man, but within a marriage, a good sexual relationship requires an effective romantic relationship. Romance is all about the *physical expression of soulful feelings.* In any marital relationship, excellent sexual functioning will depend on each person's deepest thoughts and feelings *and* the successful communication of these thoughts and feelings to the partner. Without this emotional base, sexuality loses its meaning and joy.

A Man's Role in the Sexual Relationship Is Crucial

My longtime partners in the practice of psychotherapy, Dr. Clifford and Joyce Penner, have written a wonderful book for men about their unique role in marital sexuality. The book is entitled *Men and Sex,* and the Penners have spelled out a specific set of ways in which men can get their sexual needs met while increasing the likelihood that they will meet the needs of their wives.[1]

At the center of the Penners' ten recommendations is this idea: "The most vital factor in producing a great sexual relationship in marriage revolves around the role of the man." The Penners have found that sexual patterns in a marriage begin to change dramatically when the man changes, even though the woman may be the one hindering a vital sexual relationship.

To improve marital sexuality, the man should move in the direction of the woman's needs. If a husband becomes acutely aware of as many of her spiritual and emotional needs as he possibly can, his awareness will lead to far more effective behavior on his part.

The man needs to be highly affirming of the woman's virtues, and he needs to be responsive to her leading. In this regard, the Penners strongly encourage every man to progress slowly. The image that represents the best relative pace for the two persons involves a man and a woman riding separate bicycles down a road. The woman is slightly in the lead, and the man rides with his front wheel just behind her front wheel. He isn't far behind, but he lets her take the lead.

The man needs to remain adaptable in his sexual participation, without a set agenda for the way that things are supposed to go. A man may try to get the recipe down and then follow it. This almost never works because a woman's sexual desires, needs, and responses cannot be predicted from one time to the next.

Over the course of my career, I have become convinced that marital sex can never prove enduringly successful for a man until his wife gets her most central needs satisfied. Virtually every man I have encountered in psychotherapy tells me the same story: he cannot be satisfied in the sexual relationship unless he knows that he has satisfied his wife.

In every sexual experience, mutual satisfaction is the expectation for both the husband and the wife. The woman must be able to allow an orgasm if she wants one, but the fundamental requirement for mutual satisfaction is a deep sense of interpersonal closeness and warmth.

All of this closeness and warmth, obviously, is wonderfully communicated through the various physical mechanisms of touch. When a man and a woman learn to touch each other in thoughtful and gentle ways, much about their relationship becomes positive.

Love and Sex in a Masterful Marital Relationship

Earlier this week, I talked with a couple who told me about their crumbling relationship.

"It all started when Bart and I went to his home in North Carolina," Jessica said. "It was two years ago, only a few months after we were married, and it became obvious that Bart is not comfortable with his love for me when we are around his parents. He became like a stranger. We stayed for two weeks, and by the end of that time, I felt distant and totally out of touch with him."

"You bring that up all the time!" Bart retorted with fire in his eyes. "Won't you ever let it go? I get so sick of your constant harping about what I don't do for you, how empty you feel inside, how lonely you are for some connection with me. Well, let's get one thing clear. I don't feel loved by you either. I don't feel you moving closer to me.

And if this doesn't get better soon, I don't see why I should stick around."

"Yeah, well, when you go, take that dog of yours!" Jessica nearly yelled at Bart. Then she said to me, "Dr. Warren, he loves his golden retriever a lot more than he loves me. He is certainly twice as affectionate with the dog as he is with me—"

"Maybe because *he's* responsive to my affection!" Bart shot back.

Ouch! I put a quick stop to their unsportsmanlike conduct. To say the least, put-downs and caustic comments do nothing to repair a damaged relationship.

How could two people—two people who obviously saw something attractive in each other just a few years earlier—grow so far apart so quickly? After two years of marriage, they were complaining that they had lost touch with each other—literally and figuratively. I knew where we had to start, and I knew where we had to go. We would begin with a reintroduction of the two of them to their internal feelings for each other. And we had to move to the place where those feelings became warm and satisfying again.

When their mutual feelings return, the fundamental challenge will be to help both of them learn to convey those inner feelings more effectively than they did two and a half years ago. This is a remedial course on which I have led thousands of couples. Start with your own insides, get all of that worked out well, and then you will be ready to share deeply with your spouse.

Physical touch is a magnificent way to communicate internal love feelings. But without these love feelings, the touch becomes superficial and meaningless. When the love feelings begin to return, though, it's time to focus on touching and holding. There is no better way to convey commitment and caring.

If you and your spouse have warm and committed feelings for each other, communicate them in small moments and large ones by reaching out and taking hold of each other's hand, rubbing each other's back, hugging each other every chance you get, and touching each other's face with tenderness and gentleness.

Touching can be a powerful marital communication channel. As you touch each other, you will make known your unending love and your eternal commitment to each other.

7

Let Your Marriage Soar on the Wings of Spirituality

Imagine that you and the love of your life are lying on a long white beach in Hawaii. As far as the two of you can see in any direction, you are the only human beings on this beach. The sun is warm on your skin, but not too warm. The breeze keeps you cool, but not too cool. The smell of the salt air reminds you of the immense ocean stretching out before you. You are lying in the sun on a white beach in Hawaii with the person you love more than any other, and your mind suddenly moves beyond the quality of your tan, the great snorkeling you will do later, and tonight's luau. Your brain has seized on lofty, grand thoughts.

"Look at that sky!" you say to your partner. "To think how vast it is, to think what's out there—it boggles the mind." And then the two of you pause for ninety seconds to stare into that pale blue space. "I can hardly fathom the idea that we could fire a rocket into the heavens and it might continue forever without touching any outer limit."

Your spouse jumps immediately into this discussion because it has stimulated her thinking in a profound way.

"I know what you mean," she says, still peering up into the heavens. "And they say that there's just as limitless a quality to the *smallest* of things. My friend Jeri was telling me the other day about her research at Cal Tech. Just as there is no evidence that limits exist on the vastness of heavenly space, the same is true about the tininess of microscopic space."

You ponder that thought for a moment and then say, "I read in *Newsweek* the other day that more and more scientists are coming to believe that a Creator has to be behind all of this. *Newsweek* cited new findings about the intricacies of the created order as an indication that it could not have come about without direction and planning, without someone *bringing* it into being."

"I know," your spouse says, "and the thought that a *person* is behind all this—that this person has established laws and principles that govern not only outer space, but even the happenings in our lives—that idea is very powerful for me."

"I can hardly see how anyone could argue that there is not a spiritual dimension," you say to her. "The longer I live and see the discoveries from science, the more I think that some of my childhood faith may be right on the mark."

"Do you actually believe in a God who takes some kind of personal interest in you?" your wife asks in a soft voice.

Obviously, this is the most important question you've been asked in a long time, and you take your time answering. Finally, you hear yourself say, "I have to tell you that I've been practicing my faith more lately. I haven't said anything to you about it, but I've been praying every day, praying for understanding and insight into these perplexing issues. And when I'm at the office, I've been reading the Bible some too. Somewhere deep within me, I desperately want to feel in touch with the God of the universe."

"I've been having some of those same stirrings," your wife says. "As I think about my mother's impending death, I've been puzzling over what will happen to her. Will there be some *other* life for her, a continuity of her identity? I believe there will be. Do you?"

On that beach in Hawaii, with the sun shining against your skin and the salt air reminding you of the ocean at your fingertips, you and your lover discuss what may be the most important issue in all of life for the two of you.

Why Spirituality Contributes So Much to Marital Bonding

When a man and a woman speak thoughtfully to each other about spiritual issues, their souls become invisibly knitted together. If they discover harmony in their thoughts and feelings, it is as if they together are adopting an emotional and perceptual framework for their human existence. No other dimension of marital life provides so much potential for the blending and weaving of their identities.

Spiritual understanding of critical life questions radically alters the emotional environment in which two people build their life together. The color and shape of these experiences are totally different in the context of spiritual explanations. For instance, when two persons have to face the outer limits of human life, the possibility of their own deaths or the death of someone dear to them, a mutual spiritual perspective cradles them and shepherds them through their storm. Spiritual explanations relieve a couple's anxiety during the trying times and quicken their excitement during the good times.

The very idea that human existence is not limited to what is material, that human identity may continue after the body decays, is an idea as vast and wonderful as the assumption that the heavens have no boundary. Even more important, when two lovers determine together that they believe Someone is in charge of the vastness of creation, that this Someone knowingly created them with a purpose, that this Someone takes a passionate interest in them, that He wants to be involved in a personal relationship with them, all of this adds a dimension to their marriage that nothing else can add.

In the exploration and clarification of spiritual perspective, the spouses contemplate their human condition at the deepest levels. In so doing, they create an immense and exciting realm within which they can live and die together. And within this realm, a woman and a man move rapidly in the direction of oneness. I have watched this happen countless times in my own marriage and in the marriages of the people I have seen in my office.

What Exactly Is Spirituality?

Some people, myself included, often talk about spirituality without pausing long enough to grasp how remarkable and extraordinary the very idea of the spiritual is. Things that are spiritual are not visible. Spiritual phenomena have few of the common boundaries we recognize. Spiritual power operates from beyond. It is a dimension totally different from our touchable and tangible world. It requires a very different perspective.

Ours is a society dominated by material explanations and motivations. We tend to believe in anything that can be seen, touched, proved. Although 95 percent of all people in the United States profess to believe in God, most men and women think about major life questions in a totally material way.[1]

And yet we know that God is Spirit. We cannot see God with our eyes, we cannot touch Him with our hands, and we cannot prove His existence through research or scientific inquiry. If we believe in God, we obviously believe at least in part in a spiritual dimension. Nevertheless, we may have only a small level of confidence that the spiritual side of life ever invades the material or overrules it. Our natural tendency may be to believe that our existence is largely material, and we may have only a vague understanding of spiritual phenomena.

For instance, imagine that you have a close friend who is critically ill. How do you think about your friend's illness? What perspective do you take on the necessary steps required for his recovery? If your perspective is largely material, you may believe your friend needs the best medical care, the most advanced treatment, plenty of rest, and lots of encouragement and support.

However, if you have a spiritual perspective, you may—in addition to all these material matters—assume that spiritual forces are capable of intervening and bringing about healing that is separate from, and superior to, an ordinary medical process.

You may pray to God and ask that the doctors be given special gifts to help your friend. You may ask God to maximize the healing abilities within your friend's body and to go beyond them. You may ask God to perform a special act of healing, above and beyond the normal work of the doctors, the nurses, the hospital, and the immune system of your friend.

This is, at least in part, what we mean by the spiritual. While the spiritual can be an overlapping dimension with the physical, it can also be an entirely separate dimension. You cannot see spiritual phenomena with your eyes, and you cannot prove them in ordinary ways, but depending on your level of faith, you can be as inwardly sure of spiritual power as you can be of material power. It is possible for you to be as experientially convinced of the existence and truthfulness of the spiritual dimension as you are of the material.

Since the spiritual dimension often involves the most profound issues of human existence, its importance to our lives is enormous. It has unbelievable relevance to our understanding of why we are on earth, how we are empowered, what our relationship is to each other, and what the limits are to our existence. When we fully process the spiritual dimension, we begin to recognize how central it is to our emotional and mental health. And when we more fully understand the spiritual area, it has the power to change our lives forever.

The Vital Importance of the Spiritual Dimension to Any Marriage

For a marriage to be genuinely harmonious, two people need to have similar spiritual perspectives. Spirituality involves such a huge part of life that differences in spiritual orientation can create tremendous relational stress.

A few months ago, Alan and Erica, both in their mid-twenties, came to me for premarital counseling. They had been dating for a year and a half, and they were well matched in most areas—but there was a major area of disagreement that Erica found troubling.

"I love Alan deeply and we have a great relationship, but I'm really concerned about our differences in the spiritual area," Erica said during our first session. "Alan doesn't know if he believes in a God, and God for me is as real as my mother and father. My spiritual life is an important part of who I am and how I want to live."

Alan shifted impatiently as she said this. "Listen, Erica, I've heard you complain about this many times," he said. "We've gone over all this before, and I've tried to tell you that I'm more than willing to go to church with you, to have our children go to church, and to even give our money to the church. What else can I do?"

"But, Alan, I'm not talking about going to church," Erica said. "I don't think you really believe in God. You say you don't *know* if you do, but the fact is that you show no interest in spiritual matters, and you don't even like to discuss the subject. And when your mom was so sick last spring, you had no inclination to pray for her."

Alan was clearly getting irritated. He sighed deeply and said, "Erica, you're starting to sound like a broken record! We've been over this a thousand times. We're just different in this area. For you, God is real. For me, He's not. You pray all the time, but it doesn't make any sense for me. I give you total freedom to pursue spirituality—and I'd like the freedom not to. Can't we just live and let live? Do you have to make such a big thing about this *one area* of our life together?"

Erica looked at the floor for a long time, and I thought she was deep in thought. But she had begun to cry quietly. She was obviously in turmoil over the situation. If she married this man she cared for deeply, the whole spiritual aspect of her life would have to be a private matter. How could she openly and genuinely share her thoughts with Alan? Perhaps she sensed that in time he may even try to squelch her spiritual interests, and she knew what a terrible price that would be for her.

"Dr. Warren," she said through her tears, "this is the exact reason I begged Alan to come with me to see you. Alan's right. We have talked about this again and again, but we don't seem to make any progress—at least from my perspective. What should I do? He and I have almost *nothing* in common in the spiritual area. I guess I'm asking your opinion on how important spiritual oneness really is to our long-term happiness and stability."

The Critical Questions About Spiritual Perspective

Over the next few sessions with Alan and Erica, I set out to explore the many sides of spirituality and its role in bonding and blending two persons in a marriage. I told them that when it comes to the importance of the spiritual oneness of two lovers, there are several critical issues to examine.

First, dozens of empirical studies show that marriages do best when two people have a lot of similarities. One of the most important similarities is the way two people perceive and approach the big issues of life—the fundamental questions each human being must answer.

If one partner believes everything that happens is fully explainable on the basis of practical and material factors, this approach will largely determine his lifestyle, personality, and values. If the other partner views life within a material *and* a spiritual context—including the belief that God intervenes in people's lives—this person's approach to life will be altogether different. A major dissimilarity is evident in their way of perceiving thousands of events from day to day.

But spirituality is much more complex. For instance, two people can have the same *spiritual* perspective, but they may have totally different views of God. One may see God as very demanding, even angry, while the other perceives

God as deeply caring and kind, quick to forgive, eager to be involved personally. This difference can be a gigantic inhibitor of marital closeness.

Sometimes two people differ radically on the subjective-objective dimension. One person looks for spiritual guidance in a very subjective way—through prayer and reflection—while the other person uses lists of pros and cons, analyzes every situation, emphasizes rationality over subjectivity.

Finally, two people can differ on the role of other people in the spiritual process. I know married people whose spirituality is greatly influenced by relationships with their families or other couples in their church or Bible study group. The wife, for instance, won't make a spiritual move without seeking the advice of others. But her husband is very private. He likes to climb a hill by himself or go into a closet and shut the door, and he finds the input of other people completely unhelpful. He doesn't really like to go to church, but he goes anyway because his wife finds it critical to her spiritual development.

Here's the bottom line: spirituality can be a huge difference for two married persons. If one person is deeply spiritual and the other isn't at all, spirituality-related problems can threaten the marriage. But even when spirituality is a vital part of both lives, the different ways in which they pursue their spiritual interests can be divisive.

After we explored these and many other topics related to spirituality, Erica concluded that she could not marry Alan. As you can imagine, this decision was excruciatingly painful for both of them. I had hoped Alan might come around and take a genuine interest in spirituality. But he never did, and in the end, I was relieved that Erica broke off their engagement. A disagreement on an issue as significant and all-encompassing as this one would have been like a hundred-pound weight dragging down their relationship for as long as they were together.

Five Suggestions for Making Spirituality More a Part of Your Marriage

My clinical work through the years has convinced me that for every couple, spiritual oneness is a matter of vital importance. That is why I strongly stress spirituality as a critical subject to explore for every couple pursuing marriage. I know if a couple is well matched on this dimension, their spiritual life together will provide a huge amount of positive fuel for their partnership. But if the spiritual match is poor, the negative potential is equally significant.

Sometimes couples don't consider their spiritual match until long after they are married. Perhaps no one ever encouraged them to choose a mate with whom they were spiritually compatible, but whatever the reason, they are now married, maybe even with children, and their spiritual oneness is less than ideal.

I know that two people can adapt to each other spiritually. It all starts with a desire to make this part of their relationship more mutually satisfying. With this in mind, I offer five suggestions for building a more fulfilling spiritual relationship.

1. *Explore the spiritual dimension together in an atmosphere of openness.*

Imagine how profitable it could be for every couple to have the experience I described at the beginning of this chapter—to lie on a sunny Hawaiian beach together and to openly and reflectively struggle with the huge questions of human existence.

Most people find it fascinating to discuss the dimensions of outer space. The possibility that there is no limit to the heavens stimulates my brain and stretches my imagination. And when two people openly talk about these limitless possibilities, they inevitably have to deal with matters of spirituality.

I encourage couples to take long walks in the hills, to spread a blanket along the way, to sit and chat about the weightier matters of life, to gain a deeper and deeper understanding of each other's perspective, and to discover the intricate details of personal views of the big issues.

2. *Take advantage of crises to learn to pray together.*

In a time of financial or physical crisis, two people are much more likely to find their hearts beating as one. Their personal or family needs may overwhelm their rational resistance to spirituality, and all of a sudden, they are willing to ask for help from God.

Of course, we don't need to wait until calamity strikes to pray for God's help and protection. We continually face potential crises if we let ourselves look objectively at the vulnerability of our lives. For instance, Marylyn and I have three daughters who are married to three men we greatly love. And these three couples have a total of nine children about whom we are deeply concerned. We also have tremendous affection for Marylyn's mother and stepfather. If any one of these seventeen people became seriously ill or was injured in an accident, we would be deeply affected. The time to pray passionately for each of them is *before* any adverse event occurs. Marylyn and I are totally unified in our love and best hopes for each of these persons—and this motivates us to pray for them. Our conscious concerns for all of them inspire our spiritual times together. Crises, or even potential crises, are fertile times to work on marital spirituality.

3. *Seek out a small group of like-minded persons to promote spiritual growth.*

Meeting regularly with a healthy group of five or six married couples, couples with similar challenges and goals, couples who recognize the importance of spiritual oneness in their marriages, will provide a catalyst for growth.

I encourage spouses I work with to stay close to other couples in their spiritual community, couples whose values are similar and who long for good marriages. If the group is emotionally and spiritually healthy, interaction can produce more marital progress in a shorter time than almost anything else.

4. Read a good book together.

When it comes to developing a deeper spiritual life with your marriage partner, you need all the stimulation you can get. One good source for stimulation is a first-rate book from an author who piques the interest of both spouses.

Many persons have been captivated by the writings of C. S. Lewis. His books are excellent to read together and discuss. Philip Yancey's books are similarly popular, especially *The Jesus I Never Knew* and *What's So Amazing About Grace?*

Some couples profit enormously from reading short passages from the Bible together. This reading gets them talking, and that's the beginning of building a shared spiritual perspective. I strongly recommend that couples purchase a modern biblical translation or paraphrase for this purpose, such as *The Living Bible* or the New Living

Translation. For Marylyn and me, *The Living Bible* totally changed our understanding of the Bible's significance for our marriage.

5. *As often as possible, discuss thoughts, ideas, and stirrings that come from inside each partner.*

The whole discussion of spirituality boils down to this: the world we live in, what we call the material world, largely involves things external to us—what is outside our skin. If you try to build a great marriage that focuses exclusively on the material world—house, car, clothes, career—you are likely to be deeply disappointed at some point. The foundation is too unsure, and the painful experiences of life may wash your marriage out to sea.

Spirituality involves what is inside. It is built around a quest for deeper meaning, for a clearer sense about profound and eternal matters. Marriages that involve two people who share their experiences, thoughts, concerns, and involvement in these areas of life tend to hold together and become richer over time.

Moving away from the material world and into the spiritual realm takes a marriage from the superficial to the profound, from the immediate to the eternal, from two distinct individuals to a unified couple who take each other into the inner places—the places where spirituality reigns.

The Spiritual Quest Is Significantly More Effective When Two Lovers Agree on a Path

In a poll of 756 adults conducted by *Newsweek* magazine in November 1994, 58 percent said that they felt the need to experience spiritual growth. Fortunately or unfortunately, people can take scores of spiritual paths to deal with the most profound questions of life. Quite apart from the fact that some of these spiritual paths lead to a lack of emotional and marital health, the crucial fact is that marriages can be torn apart when two partners pursue different spiritual approaches.

Because spirituality tends to emerge in the face of the most important issues of life, it is precisely here that two lovers most need to be in harmony. If one person, for instance, is pursuing a path that leaves out God completely and the other person prays to God regularly and seeks His guidance, how can this couple be anything other than distant from each other?

Having been raised on biblical, Judeo-Christian teachings, Marylyn and I have always had God at the center of our spiritual quest. We believe in a God we find irresistibly attractive. Our understanding of who God is comes from our study of the Jewish Carpenter, Jesus. In recent years, we have focused more and more on Jesus as fully representative of the God who is behind all of creation—both inner space and outer space.

The harmony we experience in this area has been a critical contributor to our marriage. What a difference it makes to us to have so much of our spiritual quest in common!

The Substantive Benefits of Shared Spirituality in Marriage

At the center of great marriages is a set of shared perspectives. The most important perspectives relate to the most central issues of life. These issues often require spiritual answers. Thus, a couple's shared spiritual perspective is critical to their sense of oneness.

Let me give you some examples. It occurs to me that the most critical life question is this: Are there a larger meaning and purpose to our existence than the few years we live on this earth? In a similar fashion, is there someone or something in charge of all this? Is there a larger context in which we live—one that offers hope for a longer future than we can easily assess?

When we lie on the beach and contemplate the unlimited space of the heavens, we are immediately in touch with our desire to understand the mysteries of life. Essentially, we begin asking ourselves, *Who is responsible for all of this? How did all of this happen?*

Our attempts to provide credible answers frequently pull us into a spiritual dimension. If the spiritual orientation we adopt is accurate, we reason, it should have multiple benefits. For instance, it should allow us to tap into greater power in our lives. It should reduce our anxiety, increase our sense of meaning, fill us with greater joy and contentment, make us kinder and gentler in our dealings with others, fill us with a greater sense of togetherness with all members of the human race, lead us to better values, and on and on.

The goal for every person and marriage is a spiritual perspective that provides all these benefits.

A Personal Word About My Spiritual Orientation

Though I was raised in a religious context, I did not develop what I think of as a healthy spiritual orientation until after I had been a psychologist for several years. This has led me to speculate that "religion" may often get in the way of healthy spirituality.

For me it all started with a careful study of the life of Jesus. When I encountered the apostle Paul's profound teaching that Jesus was the *exact likeness of the unseen God*, I decided to focus all my attention on the Carpenter from Nazareth.

I was overwhelmed with what I found. He introduced

me to a God who squared perfectly with all I had encountered as a psychologist.

I have watched thousands of persons get well when they take personally God's love for them and when they, for this reason, develop a keen and precise love for themselves. Jesus tells them that God *is* love, that His love for them is reliable and unending, that His desire is to be in full relationship with them, and that He is willing to forgive them again and again in His effort to achieve this goal.

When I began to understand these ideas, and when Marylyn and I began to grasp their full meaning, they changed our lives forever.

Get Spirituality Focused in Your Marriage, and Everything Else Will Fall in Place

Here is the last word: nothing else in your marriage comes remotely close to the importance of healthy spirituality. If the two of you begin to see all of life in light of a harmonious spiritual perspective, your days together will have power, and they will be full of meaning. You will then know what it means to have a marriage that is *one for eternity*.

8

Master Marital Conflict and Reap the Rewards

I want to ask you a few questions, and I'd like you to respond without analyzing your answers. Just give your gut reaction.

Do you think conflict in marriage is good or bad?

Do you consider disagreements between spouses constructive or destructive?

What does it say about a couple when they argue frequently?

If you view marital conflict as negative—as most people do—I hope this chapter will turn your thinking upside down. Right here at the outset, let me tell you where I'm coming from. I believe marital conflict can be a valuable natural resource for spouses who learn to manage it wisely. It can provide a steady flow of healthy energy and vitality to a marriage. While conflict is inevitable and important to any relationship, its "gold" must be extracted rapidly. Then the conflict should be resolved immediately.

If you and your partner master the skills to make conflict constructive, you will create freedom for the development of the uniqueness in each of you. Moreover, you will virtually eliminate all downward spirals in your relationship. And you will have a generous supply of energy to propel your union toward greatness.

Marital Conflict Is Both Inevitable and Important

Last year, Shannon called to schedule an appointment for marriage counseling. On the phone, this stay-at-home mom said her relationship with her husband, Craig, a high school mathematics teacher, had grown increasingly chilly and distant. She said their home had become an "eerily quiet war zone."

During our first session, I picked up on her description and asked them both to explain further.

"I suppose you could say we're engaged in our own cold war," Shannon said. "There's no open warfare, no explosive fights, no verbal hand grenades lobbed. We've just settled into a standoff, where both of us recognize the battle lines, and we stay a safe distance from them."

Craig's assessment was less militaristic, but no less troubling. "We simply don't talk to each other unless it's about the bills, coordinating rides to the kids' soccer practices, or who's going to take the car in to be fixed," he said. "We seem to fume and seethe in silence most of the time."

"Yeah," Shannon broke in, "the kids may not even know how angry we are much of the time. We don't make a big, loud thing of it. But *we* both know how frustrated and incensed we feel."

Craig and Shannon talked for a half hour about the conflict in their marriage—conflict that almost never got addressed or aired out. They freely admitted their inability to manage this conflict. They were stuck with a profound sense of helplessness in the face of their impasse. Conflict for them was not a natural resource; their conflict threatened to destroy their relationship.

It was obvious that they had to resolve the issues causing all their anger and frustration, but they first needed to learn to process their conflicts in a healthy, productive way. Without the ability to work through their disagreements and benefit from them, they would keep going around and around as if they were on a nauseating carnival ride.

I asked Craig and Shannon questions similar to the ones I posed at the beginning of this chapter: "What do you think about the role of conflict in a marriage? What's your gut-level feeling about couples who fight?"

"Oh, I think it's awful!" Shannon responded immediately. "It's *terrible* when two people who say they love each other can't get along! When I was growing up, my parents fought like the proverbial cats and dogs. Sometimes their fights got very heated, even violent on a couple of occasions. Their arguments were so disturbing to my sister and me that we would go and hide in the closet." She paused for a moment, with a far-off look in her eyes. She was clearly transported to a time long ago. "Sometimes they even argued—loudly—in public. It was such an embarrassing spectacle! I vowed that I would never fight like that when I got married."

I asked Craig if he felt the same way.

"I think conflict in marriage is sad, too, but for a different reason," he said. "My folks never seemed to have any fights, and they lived together for fifty-two years. Fifty-two! I tell you, I never saw them argue once. What an amazing relationship they had. So now I ask myself, *Why can't Shannon and I be that way? What's the matter with us?* I hate to admit this, but I've begun to wonder if we are fundamentally mismatched. Maybe we shouldn't have gotten married in the first place."

Oh, boy. I knew I had my work cut out for me. So entrenched were these people against any kind of conflict that I would have to try mightily to help them understand that disagreements are natural and inevitable in marriage.

"The first thing we need to understand," I said as

softly as I knew how, "is that all couples have conflict. There is nothing inherently *bad* about it. Craig, no offense to your parents, but if a married couple live together for a length of time without any conflict, it usually means one or both partners have given up their individuality and uniqueness. They choose somewhere along the line not to express their own desires, tastes, opinions." I looked at Shannon and said, "It's true that some people, like your parents, handle conflict inappropriately, and then it *is* destructive. Whether it proves to be helpful or hurtful depends on how it's handled—day in and day out."

Believe me, this statement was just the first step on a long journey for them. For months, they resisted any kind of open conflict, always reverting to their pattern of silent fuming—"cold warfare" as Shannon had put it. In time, however, they came to see that their unresolved conflicts were like bricks stacked one on top of the other—until an impenetrable wall was erected. More amazing still, Craig and Shannon learned how to disagree in a healthy, constructive way. Without all the emotional baggage to lug around, their marriage became lighter and more enjoyable than it ever had been.

Am I making it sound too easy? It wasn't! They struggled arduously to learn positive ways of managing conflict. Each step forward was followed by a half step back. But they persevered, and their marriage is reaping the rewards.

Why Is Marital Conflict So Frequently Disparaged?

Many married persons think that conflict is bad for a marriage, that arguments signal the relationship is in danger of collapsing. If they had their way, there would never be any conflict in their marriage.

As I explained to Craig during that first session, I've seen a few conflict-free marriages over the course of my career, and just as you might expect, every one of them was sick unto death. Simply put, if you want a marriage with no conflict, you need to marry a person who is your clone. If the person is exactly like you or is willing to sacrificially live your life instead of his or her own, the two of you may never have any differences.

But strong, robust marriages involve two healthy individuals, and at the heart of healthy individuality is the expression of unique, God-given attributes. To be healthy, every person needs to become the individual that God created him or her to be. When two married people become their unique selves, conflict is inevitable in their relationship. Each begins to express thoughts, feelings, and ideas that belong only to him or her—different from every other person on earth. When these unique differences become apparent to each of them, the immediate response may be to feel threatened. If the partners hold different beliefs and opinions, the fear may be that one of them is *right* and the other is *wrong*. If this produces defensiveness in them, the spouses may feel a need to stand against each other, to demonstrate the "wrongness" of the other. This is a typical, but totally unnecessary, way to handle individual uniqueness and marital conflict.

Too frequently, couples refuse to confront conflict, just as Craig and Shannon did for so long. They try to sweep it under the rug, to pretend it doesn't exist. Perhaps they reason that marital peace at any price means a lot more to them than marital vitality. If they make this decision, they commit a serious error. They obliterate one of marriage's most magnificent possibilities—the opportunity for two unique persons to merge their lives and to build together something far greater than either of them could have built alone. Faced with the decision about what to make of their differences, they stand at the edge of marital greatness or marital doom.

Sometimes the decision to avoid conflict is made by two people who have never learned how to deal effectively with it. If you don't know how to resolve any conflict, you may instinctively run from it. You may develop an urgent need to keep it under wraps, to quickly throw cold water on any heated moment, to speak out forcefully about how inappropriate conflict is in a good marriage.

As Shannon learned from her childhood, some conflict is horribly destructive. For instance, conflict that is not resolved quickly becomes toxic with the passing of time. Aged warfare

is a frightening enemy to any marriage. But there is a big difference between rapidly managed marital conflict and the
kind that lingers for hours and days and weeks.

Uniqueness and Conflict—
The Misunderstood Connection

In a great marriage, both persons are free to become
authentic. Within their love relationship, each can experience and express uniqueness with the support of the mate.
But sometimes their uniqueness on one point or another
will set them apart from each other. At this moment, conflict looms between them.

Herein lies the potential genius of marriage! Two
people bring the best they have to a moment and share
deeply with each other. Perhaps they differ. There is nothing unusual about that. They bring two wonderfully
unique perspectives to the moment, and their potential
for dramatic growth depends only on their ability to say,
"Let's both look clearly at our differences. It doesn't matter if one of us is right and the other wrong. The fact is
that both of us together can be enriched by this process."

They differ, yes, but the emotional atmosphere in which
the conflict occurs determines the quality of the outcome.

I believe the key component in constructive conflict is
the speed with which it is resolved. Marital conflict can

almost always be managed more successfully in what I call the *spark phase* rather than the *blaze phase*. Think of it this way: suppose a fire ignites in your kitchen. If you quickly fill a pan of water and douse the flame, little damage is done. But if the fire spreads throughout the house as you frantically search for an extinguisher or a hose, the destruction will be severe. So it is with marital conflict. Spouses need to deal together with their differences *early* in the process, soon after they have shared their unique perspectives with each other.

Here is the bottom line: healthy marriages require healthy individuals. Healthy individuals must be free to become uniquely and authentically the persons they were created to be. In certain marital moments, two unique persons will bring differing perspectives to any given subject or issue. They should feel totally free to do so. And two perspectives rather than one can contribute positively to the marriage. They should rapidly recognize the benefits and resolve the conflict without delay. Under these conditions, conflict can be enormously valuable.

Conflict Can Provide a Steady Flow of Positive Energy

I can imagine what you're saying right about now: "All this highfalutin talk about conflict is terrific in theory, but oh, so difficult to put into practice when my spouse and I are embroiled in a nasty confrontation." You're absolutely right! When Marylyn doesn't agree with me about when to take our vacation, my immediate impulse is to push my opinion with renewed vigor. "If she is right about this," I reason, "then I must be wrong. And I don't want to be wrong—even if I am!"

However—and here's a lesson for all spouses—if I perceive Marylyn to be gentle and caring with me, everything goes more smoothly.

"Just listen to me, Neil," she sometimes says with a soft voice and warm eyes. Instantaneously, she melts away my fear of being wrong, and I "just listen."

When I really listen, we often end up in a friendly discussion rather than a fiery debate. After she makes several points, I ask a question or two, and then she expands on her thoughts. Then my brain is in gear, and I have a few ideas to throw in along with hers. Sometimes she has some questions about my ideas, and her questions make me think more carefully.

When we finish discussing our vacation, we usually have a plan we both feel good about. We almost always have a far better plan than the ones we proposed in the beginning.

Conflict is perfectly reasonable—born out of two unique perspectives brought to usually relatively minor issues. Most of the things we talk about in a marriage are relatively minor. My point is that if you and the love of your life are facing a minor or a major issue, your management of it can produce a healthy supply of energy for your marriage. You may disagree at first, but before you know it, the two of you will produce dozens of insights and observations about the "right" way to solve your issue. During the process, you may walk around the issue together and look at it from different perspectives. Each may bring important facts to bear on the question. And by the time you finish, you will have a plan that is satisfactory to both of you.

Managing Conflict in a Timely Manner

Nearly everyone recognizes the importance of dealing rapidly with conflict—well before it has a chance to do serious damage to your marriage. The apostle Paul told the church at Ephesus: "Don't let the sun go down while you are still angry, for anger gives a mighty foothold to the Devil" (Eph. 4:26–27 NLT).

It isn't easy to mange conflict in a timely way. And frankly, you don't want to hurry a resolution because you can prematurely cut off the expression of unique insights that are vital to healthy individual and marital functioning.

I've worked with scores of couples in which one person was a rushed resolver of conflict. The pattern was usually the same. One partner would try to express a dissenting opinion, and the other partner would butt in, saying, "I know, I know, I know," or "Okay, okay, okay." The purpose of this rat-a-tat-tat response is obvious—to shut down the other person before she has a chance to share her perspective. But I often sensed that the shutdown came too early. An implied assumption in the "I know, I know" response was that there was no need for further explanation and illumination. However, several times I felt a need to break in and say, "Elaine, I want to hear what you were going to say." When Elaine finished her comments, it was often clear that her husband and I hadn't known what she was actually thinking.

A more common problem than hurrying to resolve conflict is taking a l-o-o-o-n-g time to achieve a resolution. This usually happens for one of two reasons. First, too many people immediately interpret any verbal comment from the spouse as probably negative. When Jackie says, "Jim, let me tell you how I view this," Jim's posture becomes like that of a boxer anticipating a one-two punch. His guard is up. His pose indicates that he doesn't want his opponent to land any jabs, and he wants to counterpunch at the first sign of an opening. Obviously, a defensive, guarded posture inhibits movement toward a resolution.

Second, one partner may be excruciatingly sensitive to *any* criticism and may interpret a disagreement as everything other than, "You're absolutely right, Jim! I see it the same way! I'm with you 100 percent!" Without this resounding affirmation of shared beliefs, the individual feels hurt and often slips into sulking and grudge bearing. The "wounded" partner seems to think that working through the hurt would be an admission of defeat, and acknowledging the other person's differing opinion as a contribution would be passing up a chance at being hurt. This need to feel hurt when your partner doesn't agree with every last thing you say is a sign of a fragile self-concept, which is frequently a roadblock to healthy, timely resolution.

The Individual Requirements of Marital Conflict Management

Don't take a detour from the direction in which we are traveling. Marital conflict can be helpful to a marriage when it allows each partner to have full opportunity to express thoughts, feelings, and views. But each person's contribution needs to be recognized and appreciated quickly, and if it is different from his or her partner's position, the ensuing conflict needs to be managed rapidly and efficiently.

To do this well, *each partner needs a strong self-concept, a well-rehearsed set of attitudes, and a quick mind and tongue.* Let me tell you precisely what I mean.

If you deeply respect yourself, you won't find it necessary for your partner to agree with you on every point to feel good about yourself. Your self-concept will be secure. You won't be in the vulnerable position of needing to control your mate's thoughts and feelings in order to feel validated. You won't need to see every difference between the two of you as a competitive event.

You may be wondering how you can have a self-concept like this. It all starts with getting the core of yourself safely positioned in relation to the God of the universe. This is the safety net I talked about in an earlier chapter. When you come to believe that you are totally accepted by God, you will be deeply secure with yourself. Your self-acceptance will have nothing to do with externals—how much money you have, how much you have achieved, or how many people think you're wonderful. It will involve what you think of yourself. If you base your self-view on truths far deeper than how you look or how smart you are, you will experience a healthy self-concept.

We have discussed in some detail throughout this chapter the matter of a well-rehearsed set of attitudes. Spouses who think that conflict is bad for a marriage won't have a set of attitudes that will guide their management and resolution of conflict.

If I reduced this list of crucial attitudes to five, they would be these:

1. Differences between us are fine. It means we're both unique, and that's okay.

2. I want my mate to be emotionally healthy. This requires the individual to be authentically himself or herself.

3. I want to hear and understand what the love of my life thinks and feels about everything, so I will listen carefully to what is said.

4. When we don't agree about something, I will assume that both of us have something important to say. I will try to express my feelings fully and accurately, and I will encourage my mate to do the same.

5. My marital goal will center on our oneness. When we don't agree about anything, I will strive to say: "Okay now, honey, how can I give and how can you give so that we can be together on this?"

When this well-rehearsed set of attitudes is combined with a well-developed self-concept, all you need is a sharp mind and an efficient tongue. Let me explain: Marylyn and I experienced what was for us a major conflict last week. We had spent the morning at an emotionally grueling, yet inspiring, funeral service for the twenty-four-year-old son of our close friends. The incredible young man was a Peace Corps volunteer in Guinea, and he died in a terrible automobile accident. We were emotionally spent after a week of grieving his death with our friends.

When Marylyn and I came home, we began fussing with each other about a minor matter. In our fatigue, we forgot everything we knew about resolving conflict rapidly. We eventually raised our voices, and I said things I didn't mean.

Marylyn walked briskly out of our bedroom and then out of our house. I immediately felt terrible about what I had said. But I couldn't swallow my pride, chase after her, and apologize. (I'm sure you can relate, so don't hold it against me—even though I'm an "expert" on these issues.)

I peeked out the window to make sure she was okay, and I was relieved to see that she was quietly watering the flowers in our front yard. I thought I would take a quick nap until she finished watering, and then I'd smoothly begin a discussion about our "mutual responsibility" for our "unfortunate tiff." But I couldn't get my eyes to close. Sleep wasn't a remote possibility.

I went to the door and said, "I want us to talk. I want us to figure out what was going on."

Marylyn didn't look at me. She never looks at me in

moments like that. But she said in a voice so low I could barely hear her, "I'll be there in a few minutes."

When she came in, we sat down in our bedroom and slowly began to work through our conflict. I said, "What do you think our conflict was about? How did that happen?"

From her perspective, the explanation was simple. She said, "Neil, you were overly sensitive, overly defensive, unnecessarily hurtful, and you talked too loud!"

I was sorry I asked!

However, when I thought about it and consciously lowered my defenses, I realized she was right, and I faced the music. I told her I could understand her point of view, I agreed that my behavior must have been hurtful, and I apologized. Then I replayed the week a little with her. As we talked it through, we both began to realize why I was hypersensitive, and I could tell that Marylyn understood more of the source of my "bad behavior." She moved over and sat next to me.

Then we began to talk through some other things that we hadn't discussed enough. She shared all kinds of feelings and thoughts, and so did I. And if you can imagine this, three hours passed without our knowing it!

We went downstairs and fixed dinner together, listened to our favorite radio program—*A Prairie Home Companion* with Garrison Keillor—and we sat close to each other the whole evening in our big chair.

That episode boils down to this: I was really mad at her, and she was mad at me. But we resolved it quickly! We did not let the sun go down on our anger. After we had talked things out, gained a clearer understanding of our feelings, and shared our different perspectives, we felt even more love for each other.

What *you* need when you encounter a conflict—and what *I* need—are a well-developed self-concept, a well-rehearsed set of attitudes, and an efficient mind and tongue. If you know how to engage in *rapid-fire conflict resolution,* your marriage can turn from miserable to wonderful in three hours or less.

How to Extract "Gold" from Every Conflict

Remember, the goal is not to simply get through conflict but to *use* it for growth and progress. With this in mind, I offer four guidelines for benefiting quickly from every conflict.

1. *Become crystal clear about your commitment to the individual freedom of both partners.*

As I mentioned earlier, you should not be alarmed if there is conflict in your marriage; you should be alarmed if there *isn't.* I regularly share with couples my strong belief that both persons in a marriage have a legitimate right to their own thoughts, feelings, and opinions, especially when they collide with the partner's views. I encourage married people to make this a major marital value: "We both have a legitimate right to our own thoughts and feelings even when we do not agree."

2. In the moment of conflict, both partners have a right to be fully heard and understood.

Admittedly, Marylyn and I used to practice just the opposite. Early in our marriage, when we encountered conflict, we set out to misunderstand each other in an effort to make our own position seem more obviously correct. The results were predictable: conflicts drove us farther apart instead of closer together.

When you feel that your spouse is refusing to understand what you're trying to say, it kills the motivation to try to understand him or her in return. More important, it prolongs the waiting time for the "mining" of all the valuable insights each person brings. The conflict looms larger and larger as the "gold" mother lode shrinks to the size of a small flake.

3. Treat both partners' potential contributions as valuable and worthy of honor.

I have little more to give to Marylyn in a moment of conflict than my thoughts, feelings, and opinions.

Obviously, the same is true for her. What I've learned over time is that what she brings often seems to become more valuable as I understand it more deeply and gain perspective on it. I now believe that healthy married persons almost always have great insights to share with each other from moment to moment.

For instance, as I have written the chapters for this book, I've handed them to Marylyn for her comments. I've never done this before. Since this is my seventh book, you may wonder why I've waited so long to seek her judgment. I think it never dawned on me that she had specific editorial contributions to make to my writing. In the past, I'd read each chapter aloud to her, and she would make general comments. But this time, I asked her to read over the material carefully and offer specific ideas.

I cannot begin to tell you how insightful and creative she has been. I have frequently experienced a sense of awe about her ability to make significant contributions to each chapter. I'll admit there have been moments when I've felt threatened that she could deal with issues better than I could. But here's the point: she brings a unique perspective to these subjects—just as each partner in every marriage brings unique perspectives to issues and problems. If we learn to appreciate this, we can "extract the gold" with greater precision and efficiency.

4. *Listen, listen, listen!*

If I am right that each partner brings a supremely valuable perspective to every moment, the only way to recognize and maximize that value is by listening. Expert listening, the kind that marriage partners need to develop, is the most obvious technique for collecting and safeguarding the gold that each partner brings to crucial marital moments.

Stop the Downward Spiral

Conflict is mostly positive in the earliest stages. If you handle it quickly and efficiently, it can become a helpful resource for your marriage. However, conflict can get meaner and meaner the longer it lurks in the shadows. What is helpful about resolving conflict quickly is that you don't allow it to spiral downward, to become more destructive, and to damage your marriage at its foundations.

It sometimes occurs to me that unmanaged conflict is like the national debt. Not only do you have to pay it back at some point, but the interest on the debt becomes overwhelming. If you and your partner have a lot of hurt and frustration toward each other—hurt and frustration that you have never resolved—it may cost a lot over time to pay the interest. When your marital accounts are kept up to date, you never have to pay an interest bill.

conclusion

A Fabulous Marriage Is Just Around the Corner for You

When your marriage becomes significantly more satisfying, every person who knows you will benefit, and you and your partner will benefit the most. Your kids and your parents will surely jump for joy. Your friends and your colleagues will be excited. The whole world will be a little better because your marriage is happier and healthier. I have often commented that our number one challenge as a society is to improve the state of our marriages. Why don't we start with yours?

After all these years as a psychologist, I can say this with confidence: *marriage is the greatest institution ever invented.* When a marriage is right, it is the place where two persons can find the finest friendship and companionship ever known, a deep feeling of security in the middle of a sometimes frightening world, a profound sense of partnership in the exciting task of raising children, a sharing of burdens in the face of endless demands and unending duties, a sexual partner with whom there are unlimited trust and permanent commitment, and a spiritual companion for mutual support and encouragement. No other institution begins to offer so many benefits—and all in one relationship. All these magnificent benefits come to a man and a woman who have developed with each other *a marriage that is right.*

Perhaps your marriage is somewhat less than right. Then what? Then you read this book as many times as it takes, and you count on my promise coming true for you and your partner. Here it is: your marriage can be at least 10 percent better in the next twelve months, and if it is, the two of you will be full of hope. Any marriage that becomes 10 percent better this year can become 10 percent better next year. You can easily see how dramatically your marriage can change and grow in the next few months and years.

Three Principles That Can Change Your Marriage Forever

Sometimes we make marriage too complicated, don't we? We analyze it, dissect it, scrutinize it, evaluate it, explore it, and probe it. My lighter-touch approach focuses on three simple principles that can quickly and effectively improve your marriage dramatically.

1. Eliminate the negative by accentuating the positive.

The single greatest tendency that spouses must resist when marital storms appear is to adopt a *problem-centered* approach to the relationship. A far more effective approach is to maximize your relational strengths, raise the value of your collective assets, and nurse your love back to full strength.

I'm not saying you should never go to a psychologist, psychiatrist, or marriage counselor when you experience thunder and lightning in your relationship, but I certainly wouldn't advise that you go there first. Read the chapters of this book together—again and again if you need to—until you start thinking more positively about your life together. Far too many divorces are the result of a professional process that essentially results in picking at each other. This national trend has to stop, and for you it can stop right now.

The key to marital growth is to rediscover all the reasons that you and your spouse fell in love with each other in the first place. Once you rediscover them, settle into a joyous pattern of living with these positive perceptions week in and week out. Be inspired together, laugh together, learn to be optimistic together, and touch each other lovingly every chance you get.

If you had a marital happiness gauge clearly visible on you, I can guarantee that a problem-centered approach to strengthening your marriage would give a low reading, but maximizing all the positive experiences in your life together would send it soaring.

I call this approach to marital revitalization the lighter touch, and I emphasize it throughout this book. The secret is to quit working your marriage so hard and stop pinching and squeezing your marital focus onto critical issues, challenges, and deficits. Learn how to proceed gently in the growing of your love, and then, like watching one of Tiger Woods's magnificent golf shots, watch your marriage soar high and far, straight down the center of life's fairway.

2. *Learn to keep your lover constantly at the center of your consciousness.*

If you want your marital love to grow, maximize the moments in which your partner is centered in your consciousness. Nothing else is nearly as crucial when it comes to growing your love. Your love is bound to grow if you surprise your favorite person with some indication that you have been thinking about him or her all day long. If you call her during the day, she will know that she is at the center of your consciousness. If you turn off the television set so you can listen to him, he will know what a priority he is to you.

There is no end to the ways you can make known this focus of your consciousness. The principle is as old as love itself: we think about the things we have learned to value most. If you are continually at the center of my mind, and if I persuasively let you know it, you will be aware of my love for you—and yours will grow for me.

A fundamental fact about marriage is that its quality depends on the richness of love between two people. Love has to do with each person's relative importance in the other person's life. That importance can be measured by the frequency of conscious focus that one person experiences for the other.

That's why Marylyn and I have each other's picture on our desks at work—so that our thoughts and feelings will be focused there. That's why we pray for each other throughout the day. That's why we send each other a surprise gift once in a while; it's as if we're saying, "This is just a little reminder that I am always thinking about *you,* for *you* are the most important person in my life by far."

If work becomes chronically more important than your marriage partner, love will wane. Obviously, if any other person comes between you, marital love is sure to suffer. There's room for only one person at the center of your consciousness, and if it is always the love of your life, your marriage will soar to the heavens.

3. *Experience your way to a magnificent marriage.*

Marriage is like a symphony. If you and your spouse together catch the rhythm of love, your lives will be a thousand times better than anything one of you could have produced alone.

The fundamental requirement of a symphonic marriage

is the synchronized experiencing of the events and happenings that contribute maximally to the growth of love. I have identified seven of these happenings, and I have explored each of them in this book. When you and your partner become deeply involved in each of these aspects of your life together, you will have a marital relationship that is rich and deep, that bonds and blends the two of you, that holds you together forever and a day.

Romance is one of these pursuits that bonds you and your love together. Every marriage could use more romance! It weaves you together, soul to soul. Here's a guarantee: build more romance into your marriage, and your marriage will begin to sing again. The rhythm of your love will become crystal clear—even in the middle of lives that are filled with interruptions and obligations.

Six other powerful experiences will move the two of you toward marital fulfillment. Take the experience of *inspiration!* Show me a marriage in which two people get inspired together, and I will show you a marriage that moves like a rocket toward the stars.

Try the experience of *touching*—gently and lovingly and consistently—and your marriage will become softer and mellower and richer.

Or make *spirituality* a significant part of your relationship. Talk together about the place of God in your lives. If you find harmony in the area of spirituality, your marriage will take on a power that will move you through every valley and carry you to the highest peaks of human experience.

If you experience *laughter* together, feel mutual *optimism* about your future together, and learn how to manage your *conflicts* thoroughly and rapidly, your marriage will grow like wildfire.

Marriage is meant to be joyful and satisfying and exciting and fun, and it will be when you build these seven experiences into your life together.

Get Going!

You and your partner have only one life to live together. Don't waste any of it. It can be such a *great* life.

Wherever you are on your marital journey, get it moving in the right direction. If you feel stuck right now, you don't have to be stuck any longer. You can catch the rhythm of love—and enjoy all the rewards of a fantastic relationship. Listen to me! Your marriage can be at least 10 percent better in the next twelve months. And if it is, your marital sails will have caught the powerful breeze of hope. You will be on your way to a human experience better than any you have ever known.

I am genuinely excited for you, and I will pull for you every step of the way.

notes

Chapter 3

1. Elton Trueblood, *The Humor of Christ* (New York: Harper & Row, 1964), 15.

2. Fyodor Dostoyevsky, *The Adolescent* (New York: W. W. Norton, 1971).

Chapter 4

1. Martin E. P. Seligman, *Learned Optimism* (New York: Pocket Books, 1990).

Chapter 5

1. J. A. Adande, *Los Angeles Times*, 30 October 1999, sports section.

2. Robert W. Service, selected from *The Speaker's Sourcebook*, ed. Glenn Van Ekeren (New York: Prentice Hall, 1988).

Chapter 6

1. Clifford L. and Joyce J. Penner, *Men and Sex* (Nashville: Thomas Nelson, 1997).

Chapter 7

1. *Newsweek*, 28 November 1944.

about the author

Neil Clark Warren is one of America's best-known relational psychologists with thirty years in his own practice. He received his bachelor's degree from Pepperdine University, his Master of Divinity degree from Princeton Theological Seminary, and his Ph.D. in clinical psychology from the University of Chicago.

In addition, Dr. Warren is a much sought after speaker who captivates listeners with his ability to passionately relate complex issues in a simple, practical, and easily understood format.

Dr. Warren's first book, *Make Anger Your Ally,* was heralded a "must read" by *Time* magazine. His *Finding the Love of Your Life* was an international best-seller and the 1993 recipient of a Gold Medallion award for America's best marriage book. Warren is also the author of *Learning to Live with the Love of Your Life,* selected in 1995 by *USA Today* as having made an outstanding contribution to the field of marriage.

A frequent guest on national television and radio programs across the country, Dr. Warren and his wife, Marylyn, live in Southern California. They have three grown daughters.